Remembrance

AND

Pantomime

BY DEREK WALCOTT

Selected Poems
The Gulf
Dream on Monkey Mountain *and Other Plays*
Another Life
Sea Grapes
The Joker of Seville *and* O Babylon!: *Two Plays*
The Star-Apple Kingdom
Remembrance *and* Pantomime: *Two Plays*

DEREK WALCOTT

Remembrance
&
Pantomime

Two Plays

FARRAR, STRAUS AND GIROUX
New York

Library of Congress Cataloging in Publication Data
Walcott, Derek.
Remembrance & Pantomime.
I. Walcott, Derek.   Pantomime.   1980.   II.   Title.
PR9272.9.W3R4   812   79–29680

Contents

Remembrance

For Alix Walcott

and

Ruth and Joe Moore

Characters

ALBERT PEREZ JORDAN, *a retired schoolteacher, aged sixty-five*

MABEL JORDAN, *his wife, late fifties*

FREDERICK JORDAN, *their son, early thirties*

MR. BARRLEY, *an American tourist*

ESTHER HOPE, *an Englishwoman, late twenties*

ANNA HERSCHEL, *an American (same actress as for Esther Hope)*

MR. PILGRIM, *editor of* The Belmont Bugle, *early sixties*

AN INTERVIEWER *from* The Belmont Bugle, *early twenties; also* A SCHOOLBOY *and* A WAITER

SET: The living room of the Jordans' house in the old section of Belmont, Port of Spain, Trinidad, in the present.

3

Remembrance was commissioned by the Courtyard Players, St. Croix, and premiered at the Dorsch Centre, St. Croix, on April 22, 1977, directed by the author, with the following cast:

INTERVIEWER	Crispin Peterson
ALBERT PEREZ JORDAN	Wilbert Holder
MABEL JORDAN	Lorraine Joseph
FREDERICK JORDAN	Monsell Laury
ESTHER HOPE/ANNA HERSCHEL	Deborah Merlin Craig
MR. BARRLEY	Frank Erhardt
EZRA PILGRIM	Charles Durant

The play was produced by Joseph Papp, and opened at the New York Shakespeare Festival, New York, on April 24, 1979, directed by Charles Turner, with the following cast:

INTERVIEWER	Lou Ferguson
ALBERT PEREZ JORDAN	Roscoe Lee Browne
MABEL JORDAN	Cynthia Belgrave
FREDERICK JORDAN	Frankie R. Faison
ESTHER HOPE/ANNA HERSCHEL	Laurie Kennedy
MR. BARRLEY	Gil Rogers
EZRA PILGRIM	Earle Hyman

PROLOGUE

Pre-dawn. The drawing room of ALBERT PEREZ JORDAN's *house in Belmont. Dark wood, a fanlight of stained glass, ferns in a corner, a couch with a fading floral pattern, a fringed standing lamp, and a large antique desk at which* JORDAN, *in waistcoat, no jacket, slippers, is sitting stiffly, hands clasped in his lap. A grandfather clock strikes four. The* INTERVIEWER *is sitting in the half dark, some distance away, holding a cassette recorder. A small microphone is in front of* JORDAN.

INTERVIEWER

Is Remembrance Day today, Mr. Jordan, seven years after the February revolution to which you lost a son, and tomorrow there will be marching in the streets of Port of Spain, and the marchers will stand with red flags for one commemorative minute outside this house . . .

JORDAN

Whose windows will be closed . . . Wait. You going to leave in the sound of the clock?

INTERVIEWER

The clock will strike again, Mr. Jordan. So we have all the time in the world. Ready?

JORDAN

Is like one of them launchings at Cape Canaveral. Boy, I sitting here feeling like a spaceman, except I taking a journey through time.

INTERVIEWER

I had it on that time. Lemme erase.

JORDAN

Not "lemme erase," boy! Let me erase. You write for Ezra Pilgrim's paper and is so all you does talk? All you young Trinidadians does so handle machine without reading book.

INTERVIEWER

Mr. Pilgrim instructed me to show you the machine, when you have to use it by yourself. Press both here for Record. Backward. Forward. Your turn.

JORDAN

No. The only machine I ever trusted was my old Raleigh bicycle. It behaved erratically and suddenly died.

INTERVIEWER

Of what, Mr. Jordan?

JORDAN

Rabies. Some rabid pothound snapped at my trouser clip and bit the bike. It's out there in the back yard, rusty as my Latin. I'm ready.

(INTERVIEWER *turns off the machine, as* JORDAN *exasperatedly paces*)

I would have written all this down, but that stubborn red ass, your editor, wouldn't hear. What about your eyes? he said. Before your memory goes, too, I'll send a boy over with a tape recorder, and if you can't write you could talk it out. Talk out what? I said. And he said, The story of your life, and I said, My life is nothing, Ezra, I have been a damn fool, and he said, Nobody's life is nothing, especially yours, and besides, I said, I cannot write prose, Ezra, I am a poet, and he said, Everybody's eyes does dim a little as they get old, but as your eyes grow dim so your memories brighten, and if you can't write prose, at least you could talk it, and I told him, You got that from Molière, because I was a schoolmaster, you know. They called me One Jacket Jordan.

(*Long pause*)

I was a schoolmaster. I was for a while Acting Principal of Belmont Intermediate. They never appointed me. A schoolmaster.

(*Pause*)

Who taught the wrong things.

(*He crosses to coat rack and puts on schoolmaster's jacket. He has become a younger man. He crosses to desk, sits down, opens a book, and recites*)

"Full many a gem of purest ray serene,
    The dark unfathomed caves of ocean bear:
Full many a flower is born to blush unseen,
    And waste its sweetness on the desert air.

Some village-Hampden, that with dauntless breast
    The little tyrant of his fields withstood;
Some mute inglorious Milton here may rest,
    Some Cromwell, guiltless of his country's blood.
    (*A cough. He pauses*)
Th' applause of listening senates to command . . ."
    (*Hands clapping*)

We'll have none of that, please. To talk in all you dialeck, I ent in the mood for no heckling this Monday morning, so whoever feel he was a listening senator applauding now, mind I ent use this ruler on his same hand for it to really smart, which is a pun in case all you didn't know. So. The page is page 43, the author is Thomas Gray. My mother, who was also a teacher, used to recite this same passage to me when I was your age, and the poem is an elegy.

(*Voices off: Schoolboys, faint, then louder*)

VOICES OFF
 L-E-G! Leg.
 B-E-G! Beg.

JORDAN
 You hear those voices? You hear those voices, boy? They grew into a rabble and they fooled my son.
   (*In the past, confidently*)
 And Thomas Gray is saying . . .

VOICES OFF
 Gray is ofay, black is beautiful,
 Gray is shit,
   (*Chanting*)
 Jordan is a honky
 Jordan is a honky
 Jordan is a honky-donkey white nigger man!

(JORDAN *whirls and seizes a ruler from the desk*)

JORDAN
 Put out your hand, boy!
 I say put out your hand!

8

Good! Good. Now turn it round!
Boy, I said to turn it round!
What color is the palm, eh? Pink.
What color is the back, eh? Black!
Well, you go learn, little nigger,
that, just like your hand,
what is called poetry, and art,
color don't matter! Color don't matter!
    (*His own palm is extended. He begins to beat it*)
So learn! Learn! Learn! Learn!

(*Pause.* JORDAN *stands there with extended palm. Then he rubs his forehead, smiles*)

INTERVIEWER

Your two best-known stories, the ones that get into anthologies the most, are, of course: "Barrley and the Roof," a satire on independence, and "My War Effort," a romance. How closely did you draw on your own experience; can we say that the work of Albert Perez Jordan was his life?

JORDAN

You could say it, if you prepared for libel. It is fiction. I always added a little truth to my stories. Pepper sauce on the meat.

(*Reads. Projection: print*)

INTERVIEWER

(*Hands* JORDAN *a small locally printed volume and announces into the mike*)
Here then, in A. P. Jordan's inimitable manner, is his last story . . . "Barrley on the Roof" . . . published in *The Beacon*, May 1971.

9

JORDAN

"Barrley *and* the Roof," boy!

(*The* INTERVIEWER *withdraws.* JORDAN *in a spotlight, the printed or manuscript page, in fastidious hand, behind him. Reads*)

Epigraph from William Blake:

"A Man's worst enemies are those of his own House and Family."

(PILGRIM *staggers in*)

PILGRIM

Correct!

(JORDAN *crosses to coat rack, changes jackets, and puts on sash and hat.* PILGRIM *begins to sing a calypso tune*)

"Run your run, Adolf Hitler, run your run. Run your run, Adolf Hitler, run your run."

(*As* PILGRIM *sings,* JORDAN *crosses to him, and together they stagger*)

JORDAN

(*Reads*)

"Whenever Wilberforce P. Padmore, part-time poet, returned home with his bosom friend, Roddy Broadwater, from lodge meetings of the Oddfellows Society, in black suits, sashes, and homburgs, whose angle suggested two irresponsible morticians, they were inevitably, indubitably, inebriated."

PILGRIM

Good night, A.P.

(*He begins to exit. Then calls out*)

See you Sunday.

JORDAN

"Once they had parted, Padmore stood under the reeling stars and, in a voice whose power ignited the windows of Belmont

and the wrath of his wife, announced to the sleeping world:
  (*Roars*)
Mabel!
Maybelle?
I
am
home!"

(*Plunges drunk into darkness*)
(*Blackout*)

SCENE 1

JORDAN

Mabel? Mabel? I'm home.

(*He flings his hat toward the coat rack, misses, retrieves, wears it*)

MABEL

  (*Offstage*)
Is only now you come, you bitch?

JORDAN

His wife replied. Charming! Padmore sneered. I should have
stayed. I'm hungry.

MABEL

  (*Enters, in nightdress, dressing gown, hat, and boots*)
Why you ain't ask Ezra Pilgrim to cook for you? Think I didn't
hear all you out in the street? Don't bother ravage the fridge,
it empty. Your son is home. Half past three, and you expect
me to cook? Why you ain't go and live by Ezra Pilgrim?

JORDAN

Well, I thought since you were up. Where you going? Padmore solicitously inquired.

MABEL

I going shopping, all right?
(*Pauses. Returns*)
And, Albert, you bound to keep your hat on in the house? You going to sleep so?

JORDAN

Padmore knew very well that he had been losing my hair.

MABEL

A hat on in the house is a bad-luck sign. Take it off, please.

JORDAN

Mrs. Padmore, when there is something or someone in the immediate vicinity I can take off my hat to, I shall. Till then . . .

MABEL

I warn you. If you come to bed like that, Albert, I sleeping in my shoes. And you can also inform Padmore.

JORDAN

Mabel! Mabel! Suppose a car knock you down dressed like that? Padmore felt a joyful fear.
(MABEL *exits.* FREDERICK, *unnoticed, enters in pajamas*)
Thirty-odd years of total misunderstanding.

FREDERICK

What's up now, Pop?

JORDAN

Frederick, you're a grown man; how old are you now, thirty-one, thirty-two? People mistake you for a younger brother on

12

those rare occasions when we are together. Now you emerge from your kiddie's room in the early hours like a kid asking for a glass of milk and a cookie, and crown it all by calling me Pop. No, wait, wait . . . Frederick, I am Albert Perez Jordan, retired schoolteacher, coasting round sixty-five years, I am bored and fed up. I am particularly fed up with you, Freddie. Fred up with Freddie. Go back to sleep.

FREDERICK

Gee, Pa . . .

JORDAN

Frederick, Frederick, Frederick, Frederick, Frederick, "Gee, Pa" is only a little worse than "What's up, Pop?" We are in Trinidad. Normal idiots might venture such exchanges as "Wha' happening, Daddy?" or "What it is Mammy do you?" but I guess it's because you're an artist. Did you paint today?

FREDERICK

Yes, Pappy. Good night.

JORDAN

Come here, son. And kiss your father good night. Don't be afraid.

FREDERICK

It's not fear. It's the after-odor of liquor that makes me upset.

JORDAN

Kiss your father, boy! There, that didn't hurt, did it? Sit down till your mom, your gee-whiz mom, comes back from riding her tantrum and tell me what you painted, or even better, bring it, that I may proffer a layman's judgment.

FREDERICK

I can't, Pop. I mean, "Ah cyant bring it, Pappy."

JORDAN

God, if there's one thing I rue, my boy, is the day I taught my children diction. I think I did it to defy your mother's earthy vulgarity. Diction has made you a misfit, Frederick, an anachronism in these days of independence. I miss colonialism. Why can't you bring the painting to Papa, Fred my boy?

FREDERICK

It's on a wall. Is . . . It's a . . . Is a mural.

JORDAN

I know what a mural is. Which wall?

FREDERICK

You ent go get vex?

JORDAN

How can art get anyone vexed? You're home on a fellowship, Fred, a grant from the Albert Perez Jordan Foundation, I am your sponsor, why should I discourage you from painting the side of the house—that's-not-where-you-painted-the-damned-thing, is it?

FREDERICK

No. It's on the roof.

JORDAN

A roof mural! Good! I suppose it's meant for passing planes? Don't you think, dear boy, that it may be a danger to aerial navigation?

14

FREDERICK

I have a flashlight. You want to come and see it?

JORDAN

I understand, Freddie dear, that in the Vatican the visitors lie
on their backs to achieve a layman's view of Michelangelo's
brush; why wouldn't I accompany you to the roof of our little
suburban mansion? Let us proceed. I hope you've signed it?

(*Exit* FREDERICK *and* JORDAN *as* MABEL *enters with a small brown
paper bag, quarreling, expecting* JORDAN *to be on his usual roost, the
couch. She closes the door*)

MABEL

Well, I'm telling you it take all my Christian fortitude to go
into Harry's All-Night Bar and Grill at four in the morning.
I have to stand up in my alpagartas listening to Harry tell me
about his boxing career, cooking with his hat on, asking me
in front of all them rum drinkers and street cleaners, "How's
the professor, Mrs. J.?" I don't call people Mr. H. or Mr. R. I
was a teacher, too, and I respect the alphabet.
  (*Crosses into the living room, removes her hat and dressing
  gown, talking over her shoulder to the empty couch. Crosses to
  the kitchen*)
Shame have you silent, nuh?
  (*Crosses to the empty couch*)
You hearing me? Where this man evaporate? Albert. Where
the hell he gone?

(*Noise overhead. She listens*)

JORDAN

Could you come up here a second, Mabel? I think our boy
Freddie's done a masterpiece.

MABEL

(*Looking up*)
Albert! Somebody walking on the blasted roof.

JORDAN

It is I, it is us. It is we. I'm looking at Freddie's work. In my layman's view, and at night by a torch, I pronounce it the greatest thing since Picasso.

MABEL

(*Shouting*)
So is that Freddie was doing up there all day, when he tell me for the last two days that he repairing the leak?

FREDERICK

I meant to patch the leak, Mother, but I got carried away.

JORDAN

Are you coming up, Mabel?

MABEL

No, I ent coming up, not with my arthritis, and the hops and shark getting cold. I go buy a plane ticket and check it out in the morning. On my way to Tobago. No.
(*Talking to herself now*)
Not Tobago, either. My sister Inez tired begging me to leave that damned jackanapes and come meet her in Brooklyn.
(*Loudly again*)
So tell Frederick Mammy will see it on the way to the States.

(Enter JORDAN and FREDERICK, *exultant*)

JORDAN

Stop the presses, call the newspaper, summon the critics, my faith in the boy is justified. Frederick, your son, has created a

masterpiece, from what I could see! I take off my hat to you,
son! I hurl it from me in the ultimate bravo! Hip hip, hip hip,
hip-hip horray!
   (*Hurls his hat away*)
Mabel! Mabel! Do you know what our boy Frederick has done?

MABEL

   Eat your hops and shark. Go back to sleep, Freddie. Your
father so bored with retirement he ent know what to do.

JORDAN

   Only one hops and shark you buy?

MABEL

   How I was to know two of you all would be up on the roof
in the middle of the night, with all Belmont sleeping, not to
buy one shark and hops?

JORDAN

   You hungry, boy?

FREDERICK

   If!

JORDAN

   Sacrifice, sacrifice, there's no reward without sacrifice. Give the
child the sandwich. I'm so excited. My advice to you, Freddie,
is to keep that roof nailed down securely. Don't leave the house
without checking it's there, and that goes for you, too, Mabel.
People are stripping cars in seconds, stealing entire buses; save
part of that shark for me, boy, and the thing will be gone.
Thank you.
   (*Accepts a bit of shark and bread*)
Harry knows I like pepper. Know what our boy has done,
mistress? He has, following the ripples of the galvanized roof,

painted what appears to me to be a large American flag. The ripples being the stripes and the holes the stars. It's a tribute to Uncle Sam. I wish my brother, my twin brother, your twin uncle, Frederick, would come down to see it. Frederick, you have exalted our house. Cheers. I forgive you.

(*Pause. Roars*)

Boy! You had nothing better to do than to spend the whole damned day on top the blasted house making me a laughing-stock again? And now you compound my embarrassment with that idiotic doodle. An idiotic Yankee Doodle? And then you turn around and calmly consume the one hops and shark that your poor mother goes out into the howling wind and pelting rain to fetch?

MABEL

It ent raining, there ain't no wind, and I didn't mind.

JORDAN

(*To* MABEL)

My mother said it when I married you—I burned out my talent in domesticity. I have wasted my life. I am going to bed.

(*Exit. Then pause. Returns*)

Buy ten gallons of turpentine and wash out that shit on the roof tomorrow. And find a *job!*

(*Exit, with hat*)

MABEL

Don't mind him, Freddie. These days, your father . . .

(JORDAN *returns without hat*)

JORDAN

I'm sorry, boy. I know what you painted. A symbol of distress. *Help us, America!* A cry from the Third World. Is that right, Frederick?

18

FREDERICK

Is just a flag on the roof, Pa.

JORDAN

Well, it so happens that it's my roof and it's the American flag.

FREDERICK

You want me to make it the Union Jack?

JORDAN

Bravo! It would at least be a monument to your father's values! It would be something that he could look up to. Today, art! Tomorrow, turpentine!

(*Exit*)

FREDERICK

You right. I'm worried about him, too.

(JORDAN *returns, in singlet and underwear, wearing hat*)

JORDAN

Furthermore, suppose they take this place for the American Embassy and bomb it?

(*Exit*)

MABEL

  (*Picks at a crumb*)

I give up hoping long ago that fool would change. When we was courting, he used to stroll with me by a place where a old coolie named Suraj used to keep ducks. The damn place splattered with duck shit, but he would hold his nose high, and as he throw crumbs to the ducks in that stinking canal, he would say, "We are feeding the swans of Avon." British from the first to the last crumb. Drunken fool. He thinks is only he who could talk English? I was a teacher, too.

FREDERICK

I know, I know, Ma.

MABEL

Primary school is true. But a teacher all the same. And a plain downright Trinidadian from Arima.

FREDERICK

Dad's got to stop dreaming.

MABEL

Dad's got to stop dreaming. You want to kill Dad? Between him and Ezra Pilgrim on Tuesday nights, they does spend sufficient to pay back the mortgage. But he is convinced that some sweepstake ticket out there looking for him.
(*Rises*)
Frederick, why you paint the man roof?
(*Pause*)
You was bound to paint God Bless America straight on top his head?

FREDERICK

I am a painter, Ma.

MABEL

Excuse me, I thought you was an artist. But since you turn house painter, you could earn some money. The whole of Port of Spain could do with a second coat. Lord, look, is morning! Go and see how that flag look by the dawn's early light; then wipe it off, Freddie, before the man get a fit.

FREDERICK
   Well, he taught me one thing, Ma: never sell out.

(BARRLEY *enters the veranda*)

MABEL
   Freddie, don't be like your father, please. Who would want a galvanize flag?

(BARRLEY *knocks. As* MABEL *opens the door*)

BARRLEY
   Hello.

MABEL
   My God!
      (*Shuts door*)
   Come in. Answer the door, Freddie.

(*Exit.* FREDERICK *opens the door*)

BARRLEY
   Can I come in? This your house? I'm here to make a deal.

FREDERICK
   I'll get the owner.
      (*Shouts*)
   Pa! A white man out here want to sell you something.

JORDAN
      (*Shouts*)
   Tell him I'm asleep!

BARRLEY
   I'm not selling. I'm buying.

21

FREDERICK
He ain't selling, he buying!

MABEL
    (*From inside*)
Frederick, ask for an excuse and come in and change, please.

JORDAN
And offer him some juice.

FREDERICK
Do what?

JORDAN
Offer him some—never mind.

MABEL
Frederick, come in and change, please.

(JORDAN *appears*)

FREDERICK
Morning, Pop.

(*Exits*)

JORDAN
"Can you help me, sir?" Padmore inquired. "Pardon my deshabille."

BARRLEY
I feel a bit overdressed for this weather, too. Are you, do you, is this your house, sir? Is your phone dead?

JORDAN
I shot it myself. You're American, are you? Why?

BARRLEY
My name's Barrley, with two *r*'s. I'm up at the Hilton. Bird watcher by aversion, stockbroker my business, and my hobby, to put it a little crassly, is art.

JORDAN
With one *r*? Sit.

BARRLEY
I phoned, but it was such a short, pleasant walk . . . I'll come rapidly to the point. I think I'd like to buy your roof. I was following the flight of a fork-tailed flycatcher when your roof caught my eye.

JORDAN
Buy my roof? The thing over my head? You Americans think you can buy any blasted thing. Buy my roof? How much? At this point Mrs. Padmore entered.
(MABEL *enters with a bathrobe for* JORDAN)
Mabel. This here is Mr. Barrley. We were discussing art, and he wants to buy the roof.

MABEL
You could wait till I come back?

BARRLEY
Sure.

MABEL
Your robe, Montezuma. Pleased to meet you. I don't mean to interrupt, but before we start talking art, you ent mind if I read you a lickle poetry I write?

JORDAN

There you are, you see? We're a family of artists.

MABEL

Is just a poetry dealing with everyday life. I will say it by heart, and I will start now. It is called, "Thy Will Be Done, Hi-lo."

BARRLEY

"Hi-lo." That an African deity?

JORDAN

It's a supermarket.

MABEL

(*Holding up one hand*)
THY WILL BE DONE, HI-LO
Rice .... Fifty cents
Sardines .... One-fifty
A chicken .... Two-fifty
Corned beef .... One dollar
Eggs, 2 dozen .... Two-fifty
Beef ....

JORDAN

(*Fishing in his pocket*)
I get the gist, dear. Don't be extravagant.

BARRLEY

I'd like to publish that.

MABEL

It don't rhyme, but is life. I think it have juice, if Frederick ent drink all, so you may wish to give the gentleman some. Kindly excuse me . . . May I see you a minute, Wilberforce?

24

(JORDAN *draws apart.* MABEL *pretends to dig in her purse, whispering fiercely*)
You know you, eh? Don't sell the damn house, eh? I want the same roof over my head tonight. Flag or no flag.

(*Exit*)

JORDAN

Socrates had his Xantippe, Samson his Delilah, and I have got Mabel. My son Frederick painted the roof. We'd better wait till he comes out to fix a price. Juice?

BARRLEY

Don't let me put you out.

JORDAN

You may be the one who'll be putting us out. Do sit. So, you collect roofs, do you?

BARRLEY

I don't collect art, sir, I collect life, and once I've acquired life, it becomes art. I like the unspoiled, the natural, and that roof's a natural. I'd have to buy the whole house, I suppose?

JORDAN

I dare say. Why not the island?

BARRLEY

It's extra-large. Maybe something smaller.

JORDAN

How about Nevis?

BARRLEY

I'll just take the roof today, thanks.

25

JORDAN
Well, Mr. Barrley, we're here to serve.

(FREDERICK *enters*)

FREDERICK
I am not selling it. I heard.

BARRLEY
I've got an open checkbook.

FREDERICK
I got a closed mind.

BARRLEY
Goddamn it, that's integrity!

FREDERICK
You can blame him.

JORDAN
The boy is a fool! He's inherited my principles! Frederick, you may never get an offer like this again!

FREDERICK
No more juice? Didn't you tell me last night to wipe it all off? Now you change your tune for some Yankee tourist.

BARRLEY
I'm not a tourist. I have papers to prove it. I collect. I collect Oldenburgs, Rauschenbergs . . .

FREDERICK
Icebergs, hamburgs, no deal.

26

BARRLEY

An artist. Your son is a genuine artist.

JORDAN

Frederick, go now and get the roof. Or a part thereof.

FREDERICK

Leave me alone, nuh!

BARRLEY

That's my boy! Struggle! Fight it! What're you picking on the kid for? Didn't you hear what he said? You some kind of Philistine?

JORDAN

Goddamn you, Barrley! Whose side you on? Frederick, every artist needs backing. Barrley is here to back you. Don't be a fool like your old man, Fred. You want to know what backing is, Mr. Barrley? Listen, nuh. You see all them big pictures they does make about African and Antarctic explorers, lost in the jungles and snows, pestered by pygmies, buried by avalanches, enduring starvation, privation, all kind of "-ation," I go tell you one thing, you hear, sir. They have backing. You know. Backing. I ent have no backing. Is me one alone out there. Whether is Byrd, Shackleton, Lindbergh, in the frozen North or the boiling desert, people *invest* in them so they could suffer and discover. Suffer and discover is my motto, too, but I ent have nobody backing me, no government, no foundation, no private interests. Is Albert Perez Jordan out there in the jungle, in the frozen hearts of men, with no gun and no blasted safari! That is called backing! Frederick, sell it. Is my house. Sell it, or I cut off the grant from the Jordan Foundation!

27

BARRLEY AND FREDERICK
No!

JORDAN
Sell it!

FREDERICK
No!

BARRLEY
Boy's got the right attitude. Integrity. Arrogance. With three *r*'s. You got my calling card, right? Here's my leaving card.
 (*He hands out cards to* FREDERICK *and* JORDAN)
Got a little jungle jingle there that sums up my own policy.
Gentlemen, want to read it?

FREDERICK AND JORDAN
 (*Read*)
"When things get rocky and things get rough,
 if the future looks like it might be tough,
 if independence ain't what you expect,
 just call the United States, collect."

BARRLEY
Remember that. Ciao.

(*He exits.* FREDERICK *and* JORDAN *tear up cards*)

JORDAN
Barrley staggered down the sunny sidewalk in Belmont, stunned with admiration. For what does it profit a man to gain the whole world but to lose his own roof? The End.

(*Enter* INTERVIEWER. *Pause*)

INTERVIEWER

One radical critic has written recently: "As amusing as such stories may be, they are perhaps the defense of a man who has avoided the realities of our society and whose only defense of his neglect lies in satire. We know nothing about the real Jordan, and had he himself faced these problems, he might have been a more important writer. He has hidden the truth behind a grinning mask that cares nothing for the sufferings of his black race." Have you anything to say to that, sir?

JORDAN

Turn it off, please. If I were to bare my torn and bleeding heart to them, would that find me favor? Do you know, do they know, my boy, what they would see? Let them look, then! All you, *look!*

FREDERICK

Hold on to yourself, Pop. Don't get desperate. Are you coming with us?

JORDAN

I'm not going. When I make a promise, I keep it, however painful. I swore, when he died, that on the anniversary of that death I would stay in my house. Tell him hello for me. I don't want to meet any of those bush-headed niggers who misled your brother standing over his grave. I'll go on my own.

FREDERICK

You've never gone. Seven years and you've never gone.

JORDAN

I've gone! I've gone! Think I'm a liar?

(MABEL enters from kitchen, bringing black tie for FREDERICK)

29

MABEL

You should put on a tie, Freddie. You ent no damn revolutionary. I won't take long to finish dressing.

(*She exits into bedroom*)

FREDERICK

You were a soldier. Come on! Lieutenant Albert Perez Jordan of the Home Guard. Come on!

JORDAN

I'll go by myself. Tell him hello for me. Tell him hello for me, and spit on the rest.

FREDERICK

Jesus. I'll go out on the veranda, I can't take all that venom.

(*Exit, as* MABEL *enters, with hat and gloves*)

MABEL

Naturally you're not coming to see Junior. Seven years.

JORDAN

I tell you never to mention the boy name in this house. Let the dead stay dead! I keep it inside me, seven years, since the blasted funeral, and you swear silence on the Bible to me, but like a damn woman you can't keep your blasted gob shut!

MABEL

You say enough. Was my damned son, too. God forgive me for saying damn! *Enough!*

JORDAN

What he dead for, anyway? A slogan on a wall? What he gone and let them shoot him for, for "Fuck You, Whitey" and "Power to the People"? You see the people crying today?

You see them going to that young fool's grave and putting flowers?

MABEL

Maybe he dead today because you was on the wrong side. Or you wouldn't take sides. Blinding yourself and believing that paradise would come, like the stupid sweepstake ticket you always buying.

JORDAN

So is I cause Junior to dead? You saying that? Your tongue is a nest of vipers, woman.

MABEL

Two o' we kill him, then. I kill him with hymns and Jesus and me scarf tie round me head like a nigger mammy in pictures, and maybe he was so ashamed of both of us, all the mockery and the way you talk like a black Englishman, that he had to go out and do something. And look how he died, just an accident from a frightened policeman in Woodford Square on the day of the riot. Albert, this country kill our son.

JORDAN

Amen, Lord, amen. And when he dead, those same two-faced niggers want to make him a martyr. They ask for the body of my son. To do what with? Play carnival and ole mass?

FREDERICK
    (Off)
Come on, Ma.

MABEL

Albert. You give them our son body and you ent go to the funeral. You and your damn pride. Your blasted damned pride. Now you can't find the courage to go to his grave?

31

JORDAN

Because is what Junior might have wanted. Because his own body would have been embarrassed to see me there.

MABEL

See you there . . . You want to know what it is we do? What we been doing seven times June? Frederick don't say anything but sweat in the hot sun and look vex. He on one side . . .

JORDAN

I don't want to hear . . .

(MABEL *opens her Bible*)

MABEL

Is just to tell you that you ain't missing no big ceremony. And I on the next side. I read this same passage that mark here: "The beauty of Israel is slain high places," and so on. Very short. Very simple. Frederick does lay down the wreath. I does close the book, and then . . .

JORDAN

Mabel . . .

MABEL

. . . and then I does say, very calmly, "Junior, your father promise he will come next year." Ten, fifteen minutes, that is all. So, wait for you?

JORDAN

Is too much pain, Mrs. Jordan. Too much. Don't make this a sad house, woman. Life marches on.

(FREDERICK *enters*)

FREDERICK

Oh, Jesus, two of you stop that bawling! Ma, leave him, come on! All right, I'm going.

JORDAN

Bawling? You find your mother and me always bawling, eh? And you, what do you do? Every year you go with her to the graveside, then you take off like a hermit to the mountains to paint. Paint? You can't fool me, boy! You run up there and hide because you can't take that memory any more than me. Than I. So mind your blasted business, that's all!
  (FREDERICK *exits*)
Lord, just let me get that blasted sweepstake and you go see my smoke!

MABEL

The daydreaming, the daydreaming is worse than when you had malaria! This man delirious in his old age, Lord! Give me the strength to walk out this house while I still have time.

JORDAN

You feel I go miss you? You think I can't manage?
  (*Goes to the door, opens it with a flourish*)
The door open. The world is yawning wide. Come on, come on. I waiting.

(*Pause.* MABEL *sucks her teeth*)

MABEL

Albert, close the door, eh.
  (*Pause*)
Albert, you standing in a draft. All right, your Majesty, when you look for me, I gone! And I mightn't come back.

(*Exits*)

JORDAN
Mistress Jordan! Do me a favor! Don't come back!

MABEL
(Offstage)
Right!

(The stage. Traffic sounds outside. A dog keeps up its frenzied barking. JORDAN goes to the armchair, and lifts up the paper. Then he puts it down slowly. He looks up to the ceiling. Then he sits. It grows dark. The clock chimes five)

JORDAN
We born alone. We suffer alone. We dead alone. Right?
(He keeps looking at the ceiling)
You know, since your own son dead, we ain't been hearing much from you.

SCENE 2

The same. JORDAN sits in the armchair. From the dark, the INTER-VIEWER's voice.

INTERVIEWER
That was a great performance, Mr. Jordan. The way you read, them characters really leapt to life. Is just one little technical-ity. If you going to move around so much during the next story, is best you hold the mike, or else we find ourself all over the place.

JORDAN
So life is, young man. All over the place.

34

(INTERVIEWER *turns on machine, speaks into it*)

INTERVIEWER

That was "Barrley on the Roof, A Satire," by A. P. Jordan, published last year. Now we go back thirty years to old colonial Port of Spain, via a story known as a pioneer work in our literature: "The War Effort."

JORDAN

"My War Effort." Yes.

INTERVIEWER

Do you remember it?

JORDAN

Vaguely.

(*Projection:* "My War Effort"
            by
            A. P. Jordan)

INTERVIEWER

It was published in 1948.

JORDAN

To heal the wound.

INTERVIEWER

What wound?

JORDAN

Never mind what wound. It was all a lie. I made it up. It happened to a friend of mine. And her name was not Hope; it was Esther Trout. I should have used Trout instead of Hope.

Hope was too obvious and Trout got away. How does it begin? "In the balmy days"? . . .

(*As the* INTERVIEWER *reads, a projection of* JORDAN *in volunteer cap and World War II uniform.* JORDAN, *listening, rises and moves away.* ESTHER TROUT, *a young Englishwoman, enters and sits at a desk*)

INTERVIEWER

"In *those* balmy days of the Second World War, I was not English, but I considered myself to be. I was a colonial, but did not consider myself to be so. England belonged to me, her heritage, her war. I adored England and there was nothing more England to me than my immediate superior at the Information Office one desk away, than the adorable Miss Esther Hope.

(*The Information Office: Morning. The* INTERVIEWER, *who has arranged the furniture, withdraws.* ESTHER TROUT, *a twenty-five-year-old, is at her desk. Above her desk a large Union Jack.* JORDAN *enters, pauses at the door. He is holding a rose*)

JORDAN

I'm awfully sorry to be late, Miss Trout, but you can blame it on the war. May I wish you a pleasant working day. May our tropic sun not wilt your English rose.

ESTHER

Your accent is almost flawless, Mr. Jordan. When are you going to be yourself?

JORDAN

I waited at the Readers' and Writers' Club last night. I have written a little poem in somebody's honor. Guess whose? I preferred not to read it. I spent a restless night wondering what happened.

ESTHER

I had to go to Government House. A reception. You . . .
Why am I telling you all this, Mr. Jordan? Now, do you want
the key to the library?

JORDAN

(Accepting key)
The library, again? Among musty tomes? Does that mean I
won't have the pleasure . . .

ESTHER

There's something else.
(She holds up a note)
What is this, Mr. Jordan?

JORDAN

What is what?

ESTHER

This.
(Reads the note)
"Miss Trout, I've adored you from the day you came into this
office. I've adored you without hope. I've worshipped you
across the gulf of race and the chasm of time. Will you join
me in a drink after work? A.J. P.S. Then marry me?"
    Is this some sort of a joke, Mr. Jordan? Because if it is, I
think it's silly. You mustn't trifle with people's affections. It's
dangerous.
(She tears up the note)
Now, be a good boy and don't get ideas. Because we're on the
verge of becoming friends. Please go to the library, Mr. Jordan.
Now. Oh, and by the way . . .

JORDAN

Yes, sir?

ESTHER

What's happened to those back numbers of *The Illustrated London News?*

JORDAN

They're being kept in my digs. As hostages. Till you agree to have lunch.

ESTHER

You know very well that they aren't to leave Reference, Mr. Jordan. Or it's my neck.

JORDAN

Passion has made me dauntless, Miss Trout.

ESTHER

The library, Mr. Jordan. There's a war on. Now . . .

(JORDAN *exits.* ESTHER *looks up from her work, rests her chin in one palm, smiles; then, the smile fading, stares as the lights fade*)

SCENE 3

JORDAN

    (*Recites*)
"Once more unto the breach, dear friends, once more;
  Or close the wall up with our English dead!
  In peace there's nothing so becomes a man
  As modest stillness and humility;
  But when the blast of war blows in our ears . . ."

ESTHER
What is this, Mr. Jordan?

JORDAN
Sorry to appear in civvies, sir, but I simply couldn't find a spot
to stash my gear.

ESTHER
Stash your gear?

JORDAN
I've joined the local defense force. I'm up for pips. Lieutenant
Albert Perez Jordan of the Home Guard. Shh . . . the walls
have ears. From a meek office lamb to a tiger on the battlefield.
I hope I'm severely wounded; then you could look after me.
I'm quite excited by it all, excuse me.

ESTHER
You've seen too many war films, Albert. It isn't like that. War's
very boring, actually. It's mostly administration. Could you
check this list?

JORDAN
We might see a little action. You never know.

ESTHER
Action? We?

JORDAN
The war, I mean.

ESTHER
In Trinidad?

JORDAN

Oh, don't dismiss the idea so easily, Miss Trout. There're submarines. There's the threat of invasion.

ESTHER

By whom, Mr. Jordan?

JORDAN

By Vichy France. They're sinking our ships. Our boys are going down. I was considered essential to the war effort here, so they didn't let me enlist. There was a rumor about a commission if I'd gotten in. At least one pip. But I doubt I'd have gotten it. Black officer in the British Army'd be a rare sight, what?

ESTHER

I'll say. Take that silly thing off and help me proof this inventory, you idiot.

JORDAN

When you call me an idiot, Miss Trout, I feel like a prince. If I wore my uniform, then would you consider going out with me?

ESTHER

The inventory.

JORDAN

Does that mean you might? I can't decipher that smile.

ESTHER

You're engaged to be married, aren't you, Mr. Jordan? That's what I hear.

JORDAN

> I am. I was. It's meant nothing since I met you. I could break it off. You only have to nod. Means nothing, really.

ESTHER

> It's meant something to me. Shall we start working now?

JORDAN

> It's all hopeless, is it?

ESTHER

> Not hopeless, but pointless. Bit of a difference there.

JORDAN

> I joined up to impress you. I would die to impress you. How about that?

ESTHER

> Don't you ever give up?

JORDAN

> Has Britain given up? Won't we fight to the last Winston said? On the beaches, on the landing grounds? We shall never surrender!

ESTHER

> We?

JORDAN

> Oh. You.
> (*Removes the cap*)
> I see.

41

ESTHER

All right. Come on: let's start on the third paragraph, page 5. Got it? What's wrong, Mr. Jordan?

(JORDAN *is staring into space*)

JORDAN

Someday, someday. We'll have our own flag. Our own wars! And the British lion will come crawling on its knees to the Trinidadian quenk.

ESTHER

What . . . is a "quenk," Mr. Jordan?

JORDAN

Oh, don't you know, Miss Trout? It's a small jungle animal pretending to be a boar. Like me. So, you may take your war, your flag, your rose, your key, and stuff it!

(*Marches out*)

ESTHER

Well. Independence at last!

(*She is smiling. Fade*)

SCENE 4

Night. Softly, sound of a tropic night. Spotlight on ESTHER *at her desk. Then, a spotlight on* JORDAN. ESTHER *rises from her desk, stretches, then sits on its edge, thinking. She takes off her shoes, then the jacket of her uniform, and rehearses a dance.*

JORDAN

"One evening, Padmore went for his usual cycle on his trusty Raleigh Sir Winston around the Savannah. Seeing a single light in his office he approached, hoping to catch a spy *in flagrante delicto*. But Padmore stood, in the doorway, unseen, and watched, in tears, with silent wonder. He knew, in that illuminating moment, that though dancer and watcher would grow old and change, the music never would, nor would the vision which the music preserved. The rose he had given her had blackened and withered on her desk, but it was there. That gave him trout."

SCENE 5

Day. Music: Les Sylphides, *softly. The* INTERVIEWER, *dressed as a waiter, sets the desk with tablecloth, a freshly cut rose, etc., in the restaurant.* JORDAN, *carrying three back numbers of* The Illustrated London News, *enters.*

WAITER

Yes.

JORDAN

Made a reservation. Lieutenant Jordan, Home Guard. Expecting young English officer to join me shortly.

WAITER

I hope he reach shortly. Is wartime, you know, and it have blackout and curfew.

JORDAN

I know. When it tolls, we'll depart.

WAITER
Eh? Oh ho!

(*Enter* ESTHER. WAITER *seats her*)

JORDAN
(*Presenting magazines*)
The hostages. As promised.
(*Pause*)
I love you, Esther. I love you and I'm afraid.

ESTHER
Will you stop it?

JORDAN
All right.
(WAITER *exits*)
Once you know it, that's all.

ESTHER
I was afraid you were making a fool of me, do you understand?
Listen to that, *Les Sylphides*. I used to dance to that. Me, a
sylph. I should starve. I'm getting too fat, living off the war.

JORDAN
You're a ballet dancer?

ESTHER
Was. War stopped all that. Glad they've turned it off. But
somebody here's very chic, my dear. I came because I thought
it was time we had this all out. No more little games. I hate
flirtations. We aren't a very frivolous race, the Brrr . . . itish.
So your little notes were very annoying. Not at all flattering. I
thought: Who is this foolish man? I'm younger than you,
Albert, but I've seen more. Mind my chattering? I think it's
for our good, you see.

JORDAN
   Oh, no, no, go on.

ESTHER

   Everybody's got sad stories about this war, so I shan't tell you
   mine. Just swiftly, British manner. Both parents. I've none,
   shall we say. No, no. It's our war. It's just Europe ripping its
   own guts out again. It did it before, with my dad. So I've been
   alone a lot. Lost a fiancé on the *Ark Royal*. Just a boy, but lost
   all the same, so I asked to be posted out here. I've grown to
   love it here. You mustn't make fun of that. Albert, I think
   you're a silly, affected, but lovely man. You've pestered me
   relentlessly for three months. It's been worse than the Blitz.
   And I've thought very carefully about this, all the possible
   complications, but if you want me to, I'll marry you.
      (*Silence*)
   I see. What's her name, Albert? Your fiancée?

(*Silence*)

JORDAN
   It doesn't matter, does it?

ESTHER

   I'd just like to know who I lost you to. I think you should leave
   the office, don't you? Either that, or I do.

JORDAN
   Excuse me, love. Men's room.
      (*Exits. He turns and walks toward the armchair, reciting from
      memory*)
   I went to the men's room for twenty years. I never saw Esther
   Trout, I mean Esther Hope, to talk to again. I never went
   back to the office. Not even for my things, until I heard that
   she had gone back to England. To their war. A mortal error.

45

To stay within the boundaries of my race and not cross over, even for love. Esther! I'll never look upon her like again. Since then I have been a mind without a country. From that day onward I have always known my place. The end.

Well, did you prefer that story, Mr. . . . I've forgotten your name. No, no, it'll come back. Roberts . . . R . . . R . . . Your face . . .

INTERVIEWER

Rogers, sir. You taught my father.

JORDAN

Ah, yes. There were two Rogerses, about your father's age; one was rather timid, and one was dim-witted but excellent with his hands. He runs a garage.

INTERVIEWER

That's my father, sir.

JORDAN

Not dim-witted exactly. Just that he hated books. I remember he built us an excellent cabinet. I loved him. I loved them all, you see. Is he doing well?

INTERVIEWER

Just well enough, sir.

JORDAN

Rogers's garage, of course! Tell him One Jacket sends his love and ask him if he recalls making that cabinet.

INTERVIEWER

I shall, sir.

JORDAN

He had an amusing cranium.
(*Demonstrates*)
The others called him Mango Head, and I'd, oh, how, how
it all comes back so clearly, I'd stroke . . . he had a funny
dent right here, like a cleft crown, ha ha! And I'd say, "Did
you learn so and so, Mango Head," and give it a little rub, and
he'd grit his teeth in rage. Oh, he was a lovely boy. Tell him
about that cabinet, you hear, don't you forget now, and tell
him that One Jacket says he's got a fine son.

INTERVIEWER

Yes, sir. Shall we continue . . . ?

JORDAN

Don't know what happened to the other Rogers. I sent them
out into the world, frail, confident things. To have that happen
every year. Every year. It broke my heart. You look a little like
my son. The longer you stay in this house, the more you re-
semble him.

INTERVIEWER

That was one of my questions, sir. Everybody in Trinidad
knows what happened. How come you have never written
about it?

JORDAN

Because . . . It is a subject for thunder, not for me, a mouse
with a fountain pen. You must go now. My memory is so
strong, Master Rogers, that I confound the living and the dead.
Reading those stories had the power of incantation. They
sounded real, and now I find reality hard to bear. I'm afraid
of the power of the resurrecting word. Go, and come back some
other morning, thank you. That machine contains their voices,
and it's strange.

INTERVIEWER
Goodbye, sir.

JORDAN
Good morning, Master Rogers.

(INTERVIEWER *rises, exits.* JORDAN *remains in the living room. The* INTERVIEWER *passes* ANNA HERSCHEL *at the front door; she is carrying a baby.* ANNA *sits on a veranda chair, tired. Then rises, hesitant*)

JORDAN
He's left the book behind. How's he going to do his homework?
(*Acting out young* JORDAN *and young* ROGERS)
Where's your book, Mango Head? How can you do your homework without your book?
(*As young* ROGERS)
Ah leave it home, sir. It lose.
(*He laughs. Opens the book, reads*)
"A mortal error. To stay within the boundaries of my race and not cross over, even for love. Esther! I'll never look upon her like again."

(*The front door creaks open wider.* ANNA HERSCHEL, *a young white woman, stands in the doorway, carrying a sleeping baby on one shoulder, a bag slung over the other.* JORDAN *does not turn*)

ANNA
Can I come in?

JORDAN
I'm so glad you came. I'd given up, Trout. Sometimes I say Trout instead of Hope. It's a little joke of mine. It's a game you might play sometime. Come in.

(*Fade*)

Act Two

SCENE 1

The same. The drawing room, next morning, JORDAN *in a floral, tasseled dressing gown,* EZRA PILGRIM *sits on the couch, a bottle of rum and a soda near him. He drinks.* JORDAN *watches patiently.*

JORDAN

Love never dies, it stays the same.

PILGRIM

I can't face Monday without at least two of these, boy, as you know. Nah, nah, don't worry, Al. It ain't the poem. Right. Read. Read.

(JORDAN *offers him the bottle*)

No, no, I done, no more. You could move the bottle.

JORDAN

(*Recites*)

"Love never dies, it stays the same;

though lovers die, the more Love grows

in others with a different name,
it is their heart's immortal rose.
A vision from across the years,
although sons die, and friends betray,
waters this rose with joyful tears.
Ah, Hope, that never went away
but hid within me all this while,
when sons have died and friends betray,
you greet me, at the closing day
with that forlorn, forgiving smile.
                    A. P. Jordan"
  (*Pause*)
What's the verdict, Pilly?
  (*Pause*)
You know I can take it.

(PILGRIM *pours another drink*)

PILGRIM

It kinda Christmas-cardish. Or, worse, is like one of them things at the back of the paper with a very dim photo of the deceased, but the author is A. P. Jordan, so I'd be mad to turn it down. What's the title?

JORDAN

"Remembrance," and put for the dedication: To E.T. No, put: To A.H., just under the title; that is, if the measly eight dollars and fifty cents you pay not going break your budget. Christmas card? You know the best Christmas-card writer? William Blake. Take it or leave it, that's how I feel. Maybe is not modern enough for your little pseudo-radical rag, but that's the best I can do.

PILGRIM

I told you, I go print it with pleasure, Albert. Is Monday morning, so don't give your old pardner a hard time. I am the one who respects your work, especially the short stories, and I told you one day I'll send a boy around with a tape to take down your reminiscences. Because your eyes. This thing kind of close to the bone, boy. What is this "friends betray" business? Which friends?

JORDAN

Look, Ezra Pilgrim! You think you're my one friend? Blasted conceit! All right. You are. Is just a bloody poem.

PILGRIM

"Sons die." That ain't just a bloody poem, Albert.

JORDAN

Look, Ezra, I know your big ambition was to be a barrister, but I too old for you to practice on, you hear? Friends betray, and that's it! Sons die, and that's also it. That's eight dollars and fifty cents' worth of truth.

PILGRIM

You talking about my so-called influence on Junior, right? Because I let him loose in my library? Because I made him read Césaire and Marx and Fanon? That was wrong?

JORDAN

I am talking about life. Life, man, life!

PILGRIM

Because I let him write those articles in *The Bugle?*

JORDAN
Ezra . . .

(PILGRIM *goes for the bottle*)

PILGRIM
Life? I'm a confirmed bachelor, Albert. I haven't had your good luck, so the only family I've ever had is this.

JORDAN
You're not that unlucky, Ezra, you nearly succeeded in stealing away my son. Put down the damned bottle.

PILGRIM
Junior?

JORDAN
Aye.

PILGRIM
Stealing your son? Ahh . . . that's what the poem is all about, then. That "friends betray" business. I best have another one, Albert, because . . .

JORDAN
Face the truth, Ezra. It's time. We avoid it, avoid it, face the truth. That poem is the truth . . .

PILGRIM
I tried to steal your son.

JORDAN
My friend . . .

PILGRIM

What is it I was supposed to have done? Help kill that boy?
I was Uncle Ezra to him.

JORDAN

And I was Uncle Tom. I was his father, and I was also Uncle
Tom. You printed all his revolutionary stuff in *The Bugle*,
because you were scared shitless, Ezra; you recanted on all the
culture we had known. Remember what we were, and what
principles we considered sacred, friend?

PILGRIM

I thought I was an editor, but this is news to me, that I'm a
murderer, too. Jesus, you've called me many things, Albert,
but never this one. Jesus.

JORDAN

Shhh. You'll wake the child.

PILGRIM

What child?

JORDAN

Never mind. Just don't start shouting. I have a child in there.

PILGRIM

I hope Mabel don't hear about it. Is there somebody in there,
Albert? You have some girl in there 'cause Mabel's gone? Well,
that is your business, but I'm not going around, I'm not leaving
this house carrying that guilt inside me about Junior. I will
not. You hear?

JORDAN

Keep your voice down, please. They shot him, Ezra. They put a hole in that boy's body, but they've ripped out a hole in my own heart that nothing, nothing can fill.

PILGRIM

A stupid, excited policeman shot him, it wasn't "they"! The country was under martial law.

JORDAN

Bad company, bad company. What was the company we kept in our youth, Ezra? The company of great minds, great music. Right, Pilly? So we educated ourselves past ourselves, eh, Pilly boy? While our contemporaries were out chasing woman, drinking grog, and sniffing like dogs round the arse of a pension, we'd be here after work, right here on this veranda, right there by the seed ferns, way past suppertime, reading Macaulay, Carlyle, and Edward Bulwer-Lytton to each other. Yes, friend. A. P. Jordan and young Ezra Pilgrim civilized themselves.

PILGRIM

Belmont is a village, Albert, so think of it this way: that your son, Albert Perez Jordan, was the village Hampden.

JORDAN

The boy was wild, Ezra. He called me a Fascist, but the boy was wild. He ran with wild companions, wild ideas. He said I ran this house like a classroom, but discipline was always my weakness since the army. Sometimes I feel I could beat this whole damn country with a strap, ministers and all! Big boys!
(Mime)
"What wrong with the phone, eh?" WHAP! "Who lock off the water?" WHADDAP! But the boy was wild. Pilly, I'm sorry.
(Pours PILGRIM a drink)
But I want to show you something.

54

(*He is at the record player*)

PILGRIM

Goddamnit, man, Albert, I can't stop and listen to no music now.

JORDAN

The house quiet, Mabel ain't here and Frederick's gone. Every anniversary of Junior's death, he goes on one of his periodic retreats to the hills, you know that.

PILGRIM

Albert, look! I know you're retired and you want a little company, but Monday is a bitch of a time in the printery, so I'll pass in after work, so if you ain't mind, le' me just take this poem.

JORDAN

Not "lemme" just take. Let me just take.

PILGRIM

Let me just take. I can't take the classics before lunch.

JORDAN

You printing it just so? Without asking who A.H. is?

PILGRIM

Yes, I printing it, Albert. I'm concerned with the part that concerns me, but I'll print it. So, I gone.

JORDAN

Ask me.

PILGRIM

Ask you what, man? 'Tain't my business.

JORDAN

Don't shrug your blasted shoulders at me, Ezra Pilgrim!

PILGRIM

Yes, teacher! I unshrug my shoulders. So, who is A.H.? Hitler?
(*Sings*)
"Run your run, Adolf Hitler, run your run."
(*Pause*)
Albert, I fainting with curiosity.

JORDAN

Prepare to faint with shock, old friend. A girl came into this
house last night. A girl from off the street—so drugged with
tiredness that she's slept in there for hours, except when she's
had to change or feed her child—standing there on the veranda
near the ferns. An American, a drifter. I've feasted my eyes on
them asleep in Junior's room, and her name is Anna Herschel.

PILGRIM

So I can go now.

JORDAN

I've gone around the house on velvet feet. I warned the sun-
light entering her room not to make a noise. I wanted her to
sleep after thirty-five years of wandering among the ruins of
bombed-out London. She said to me, last night, before she
went to sleep, jokingly, "Maybe I'll dance for you sometime,"
like Esther, Esther Trout? Believe me, Ezra, she is Esther
Trout.

(ANNA *appears from the bedroom*)

PILGRIM

I see. Hello. Remarkable.

ANNA

Hi . . . I didn't know . . .

PILGRIM

Hello. Good morning.

JORDAN

Anna, my dear friend and editor, Ezra Pilgrim.

ANNA

Heaven, I'm in heaven. Joke.

JORDAN

You slept forever. Ezra here's a rabid balletomane and an
armchair conductor, like me. He sits here Sunday mornings
with the bottle open and his eyes closed, conducting. I'll turn
it up . . . Would you dance for Mr. Pilgrim?

PILGRIM

Albert . . .

ANNA

Hooo, wait, wait, hold on! Would I what? I thought there'd
be a catch. What kind of dance? That's Chopin.

JORDAN

We so rarely get a chance down here, you see. I thought . . .

ANNA

You're crazy. Sorry. I mean . . . Oh, shit, I'm a mess. Excuse
me. That was a little joke on myself last night, about dancing.

JORDAN

Oh, I know. It wasn't your promise. I thought you might have brought a little delight, joy, purely spiritual joy to the hearts of two old men . . .

ANNA

Dance. I had a baby. I haven't danced . . . not ballet anyway; it's eight-thirty or something . . . in the morning.

JORDAN

I'm sorry. The way I put it sounds a little obscene . . .

ANNA

Is Mrs. Jordan back? I'd love to thank her.

JORDAN

She's gone.

ANNA

Gone. Aha . . . I see. I'm awfully sorry, you understand, Mr. Pilgrim, but I wasn't such a hot dancer anyway, you know. Just an Off Off Off Broadway gypsy . . . And nothing you ever do or say could ever be obscene, Mr. Jordan . . . Ever.

JORDAN

It was just one of my selfish, crazy impulses, that's all. Sorry. You better go to work, Pilly. God, I feel lecherous and soiled.

PILGRIM

It was nice to meet you, Miss . . .

ANNA

Call me Anna. I love Trinidad. I think you're lucky to be in such a beautiful country and have such a beautiful friend as Mr. Jordan.

JORDAN

Go to work, Pilgrim.

(ANNA *goes to the record player and bends to start the record*)
No. If you do that, Miss Gypsy, it will seem an obscene request.

PILGRIM

Shut up, Albert, we all understand . . .

JORDAN

. . . and I was not in quest of an obscene experience, but I simply wanted, because of the beauty and strength of this morning, to show my friend here that there is still innocence and grace left in this sordid world of ours and . . .

ANNA

Sit down please, Mr. Pilgrim . . . Now, there's a legato passage here that I can manage better. What the hell.
(*She turns the record over to a slower movement*)
Just make yourselves invisible and I'll try . . . it's like the legend of Susanna and the Elders, except they were just old Peeping Toms. And it's not like an audition here, because I'm happy and, oh, cut it out and do it, lady . . .
(*She begins to dance,* PILGRIM *looks on, then begins to applaud*)
No, no, don't applaud, it's terrible! Terrible!
(*Stops*)
Turn it off. Please. *Please turn it off.*

JORDAN

It's beautiful . . .

PILGRIM

It was a wonderful experience. One that an old man will always cherish. I saw Pavlova once in London

(ANNA *ransacks the record rack, selecting, then holds up record*)

ANNA
> Whose is this?

JORDAN
> My son's. Junior's or Frederick's.

ANNA
> Well, this is more my speed. If I'm going to earn my keep.
> (*She puts on a heavy rock number. Moves wildly, as a disco dancer*)
> *Sit back, gentlemen, and enjoy the ride!*

JORDAN
> Stop it! No! Better her dead than this. Better her dead than this! What have they done to you, Esther? You didn't have to punish yourself.

ANNA
> I didn't want you to get the wrong impression. I'm no saint, Mr. Jordan.

PILGRIM
> Nobody is, kid.

JORDAN
> "Nobody is, kid!" Stop trying to talk Yankee, Pilgrim. And isn't it time you went down to work?

PILGRIM
> I saw Pavlova once, in London. She moved like a young birch tree in moonlight. For a second there . . .

ANNA
> Thank you, but I'm not Pavlova, Mr. Pilgrim.

(*They shake hands*)

PILGRIM

Bless you, Anna. Watch out for him. He's dangerous. He sits there like an old spider in a chair, spinning remembrance. So long, Al.

(*He exits*)

ANNA

He's a nice man. You have nice friends. Boy, am I rusty. Uh!

JORDAN

Do you feel used?

ANNA

Used. Oh, no, not at all. There was a shaky second there when it felt a little . . . you know. You start . . .
   (*Pause*)
Forget it. Let me just be thankful for some peace. You've never asked me who I was.

JORDAN

I knew who you were.

ANNA

Yeah? You know more than me, then. You don't care? Pretty insulting. I didn't know it showed. I'm not tough, I just talk tough. Jesus, I never slept so long . . . You know, you start bright and confident, star of some small-town company, then you get the first shock, you're one of five thousand, and then you start to take revenge on your ambition, and soon there's a baby with the father gone. And there's an ad saying "Dancer Wanted," and there you are, Pavlova from Rhode Island doing the Funky Chicken at ten in the morning with two stars on your tits under the red lights of an empty bar in Jersey, but what the hell, you're dancing.

JORDAN

All artists make compromises, love. Don't cry like that. Make a sound.

ANNA

I came out of that bar in Jersey in freezing sunshine feeling so soiled, so ashamed of degrading myself, that I borrowed all the money I could and went to a ticket office and said: South! The farther the better, and this is the farthest the ticket went! I should shower. I'm ready to move again. I'm going to leave very soon, Mr. Jordan, soon as I get that money wired to me. But in the meantime, I am very grateful. Very. You're like a saint or something, you know that?

JORDAN

I'm not.

ANNA

You've never asked who I am.

JORDAN

I thought I'd let you tell me in your own good time. If you wanted to. And you don't have to tell me now.

ANNA

Next to you, I'm a coarse person.

JORDAN

You'll be a great woman. You'll be a great dancer. One day you'll be famous, and at least I can say, "Anna Herschel danced in this house."

ANNA

I don't believe in that any more. Fame and all that. I mean, I think it's okay if you're famous inside yourself. You know? You don't have to get reviewed.

JORDAN

I know.

(ANNA *rises, paces*)

ANNA

Don't say I know. 'Cause you don't. Sorry. But you don't know shit. I'm sorry. But it's so easy to let it all slide and not give a fucking shrug when you hit bottom. When you asked me to dance I thought, Yeah, yeah, sure, like seeing yourself in a dirty mirror. It was Eighth Avenue all over, the Raincoat Brigade. I been in every cause, I was a permanent extra in all those crowd scenes—free-thinking, free-screwing Anna. Know what I thought? Jesus, I got to clean my mind.

JORDAN

Anna, you're too hard on yourself.

ANNA

Not hard enough. That's who I hate most: me. I waited for that door in there to open. Paid a landlord that way once. That's the way it's always been, nothing for nothing. I sound like a whore. I'm not a whore. I'm just down to the only legal tender I can deal in.

JORDAN

My dear . . . my dear . . .

ANNA

I'd like to be able to trust people again. I once laid it all out to a guy, I mean, my self, not my body. Offered it to him on a platter . . .

JORDAN

You bared your soul to him, and he was terrified and walked away. It's an old story, isn't it?
(*Pause*)
Can you do an English accent?

ANNA

Me? Nah. No way.

JORDAN

Ever tried? Acting one, perhaps?

ANNA

Couple times, I guess. In fun. 'Tisn't very good. Why?

JORDAN

Would you say: "I've grown to love it here. You mustn't make fun of that . . ."

ANNA

In an English accent? I'd be awful.

JORDAN

Oh, try it. Once. For me?

ANNA

(*Giggling*)
I'm a dancer, I'm not an actress.

JORDAN

Give it a try. "I've grown to love it here. You mustn't make
fun of that . . . Albert."

ANNA

Okay . . .
  (Giggles)
"Oi've grown to luv it ere, you mustn't . . .
  (Cracks up, laughing)
Too cockney, huh?

JORDAN

What's your religion?

ANNA

None. Why?

JORDAN

Will you come closer, please?

ANNA

What's all this about? I just danced.

JORDAN

  (Crooked arm extended)
Will you, please?

ANNA

This is tougher than paying the rent.
  (Takes his arm)
I must be crazier than you are to do this. What do I do next?

JORDAN

Face the light. Where there's Trout, there's Hope. And be
still. Hang your head in blushful shame, my dearest; no, tilt
that chin upward in defiant pride.

ANNA

Defiant pride.

JORDAN

I sorry we get here twenty years late, Reverend Rabbi, but I had a little bladder trouble and a serious attack of cowardice, not to mention colonial inferiority, but we here now, anyway.

ANNA

Defiant pride is killing me.

JORDAN

So if you could get through your semi-demi as fast as possible, I'd be grateful to you for restoring my honor, for keeping my promise, and you best make one thing of it—like christening the child, pronouncing this business null and void one time— because bigamy is still a serious charge, ask Mabel, and with modest lechery, you may kiss the bride.
(*Turns to* ANNA)
I have kept my word, haven't I?

ANNA

Someone you loved, huh?

JORDAN

During the war.

ANNA

Are you in touch with her?

JORDAN

I'm talking to her. Oh, that's nonsense. She died, you see. She died in a swimming pool from a heart attack in Coral Gables,

Florida, trying to extricate herself from a rubber tire. Life is ridiculous.

ANNA
  I'm sorry.

JORDAN
  Am I forgiven?

ANNA
  Yes. Will I get to meet Mrs. Jordan?

JORDAN
  You'll meet her. Mabel, my monument. And you'll love my son Frederick, I know that. He has his mother's heart.

ANNA
  His paintings, they're weird.

JORDAN
  Modern art. It's him they should have shot for that shit.

ANNA
  You don't mean that. I'm going to take the baby for some air. Do you want to come?

JORDAN
  It would look a little incongruous, don't you think?

ANNA
  Why?

JORDAN
  Don't you think so?

ANNA

Certainly not. I'd love you to. Come on.

(FREDERICK *enters the veranda with his painter's knapsack and a rolled canvas*)

FREDERICK

(*Reciting*)
"Once more up to the beach, my friends, once more,
And lie there till your naked arse goes red . . .
In peace . . ."
(*Spoken*)
I'm home, Professor. I'm home, and I'm hungry.
(*Enters*)
Well, what have we here?

JORDAN

Frederick, this is Anna Herschel. Anna, Frederick.

FREDERICK

Anna Herschel.

ANNA

Hello.

JORDAN

Anna's a great dancer.

ANNA

Not really. Your father's been very kind to me. I got tired and lost and I . . .
(*To* JORDAN)
Sounds phony, doesn't it?

FREDERICK
Do you like painting, Anna?

ANNA
I don't know much about it.

(*The baby cries*)

FREDERICK
What's that?

ANNA
It's a baby . . .

FREDERICK
Yours?

ANNA
(*Nods*)
Mine . . . I was just going to take him out . . .

FREDERICK
He's in Junior's room. That's great. It's been empty. Come on, come on, you take him out, and I'll walk him. It's a him? I'll walk him with you and I'm going to bore your ears off about my painting, unless I'm stealing you from the old man. Am I stealing her from you, Professor?

JORDAN
Steal her with my blessing. I thought you were hungry.

FREDERICK
Professor. How can you talk of food at a time like this? He's got no poetry in his soul, Anna. He's a Philistine. Come on,

let's go. I'll put these things inside. I been up in the mountains, you know . . .

(*He embraces* ANNA *as they exit.* JORDAN *puts on the record, the volume low, listening. Fade*)

SCENE 2

The same. Morning. A week later. MABEL *at the window,* JORDAN *resting in the armchair.*

MABEL

Albert, you too young for me, you hear? For seven days I gone to catch some rest in Princes Town, and in those seven days you not only pick up some young chick but you contrive to have a baby, too? Is only the Almighty who did so much in one week. If you keep this up in your retirement, you go kill me from surprise.

JORDAN

Well, it's you who left me, old queen.

MABEL

I came back, yes. But I didn't come back for this: to look through my window and see some hippie and my last son strolling arm in arm like man and wife in that park. I go put up a sign, you hear? JORDANS' REST HOME.

JORDAN

Arm in arm? Let me see.
     (*He walks over to the window, and after a while puts his arm around* MABEL)

Seven years ago they could have been killed. Maybe there's trout.

MABEL

Why you let this girl in, Albert? How she could confuse you so?

JORDAN

I told you. She used her last cent to come out here with the child, to get to the farthest point that she could, to the end of the world.

MABEL

Belmont is the end of the world?

JORDAN

She was supposed to meet friends here. Somewhere in this neighborhood. But it was either an old or a wrong address and she had no money for a hotel. The plane was four hours late, she got as far as a taxi could take her, and she got out and started walking.

MABEL

Then she looked through this window and saw the Pope of Belmont shining through the glass, and lo and behold! we have a boarder. She ha' to go, Albert. And you know that. Frederick is the anchor she using to stay here.

JORDAN

Listen, Mabel.

MABEL

And I been watching you. You like her, too, don't you, Albert?

JORDAN

Too? What you mean?

MABEL

You think all I do is cook, sing hymns, and tolerate your moods. You think I don't read? You think I ain't realize who Padmore is? You think I never read "My War Effort," and realize that if you wasn't such a coward thirty years ago, you would of leave me? Well, the way I have watched you watching her, all I can see is memory and regret. Lord, I ain't know why I had to come back for this.

JORDAN

Woman, you imagining things. Is you should have been the blasted writer.

MABEL

You think what you have written, however long ago it is, the book still there, you can't kill a book, you think it didn't hurt me to look like such a fool. You write some hard things, Albert. My mother said it when I married you, I burned out my talent in domesticity. I have wasted my life. Whether is "Barrley and the Roof" or "My War Effort," think they didn't hurt me?

JORDAN

I didn't mean to hurt you, woman. I just was not good enough. That was what makes my work so small. I am a small man, Mabel.

MABEL

Anyway, like I always told you, is never too late to find somebody young, however different. So, if when I wasn't here you and she had anything going on, don't let me stand in your way. I have always felt, you have always made me feel, that I stood in your way.

JORDAN

In my way? Where you think I would be today, woman? In a rum shop somewhere quoting Shakespeare and Macaulay to a bunch of no-teeth drunkards. I never been great enough to write about the simple things, about real magnificence, about you, in fact, my dear.

MABEL

I ain't want no magnificence, Albert. I just want to go to my grave in peace, knowing that I didn't stand in your way as a writer. And to see that love in your eyes coming back again so fierce as if you wish you was young and could go away with her . . . I can't take it.

JORDAN

Mabel. We ain't do nothing in this house. I would not violate a memory. Is very simple. Listen, Mabel: William Blake:
    (Recites)
"To Mercy, Pity, Peace, and Love,
  All pray in their distress;
  For Mercy has a human heart
  And Peace, the human dress . . ."
    (MABEL exits)
So cherish Pity, lest you drive an angel from your door . . .

(FREDERICK and ANNA, carrying the baby, come in)

FREDERICK

Hi, Pop.

ANNA

Hello, Mr. Jordan. I'll just see how he is.

(She exits)

FREDERICK

Had a nice little walk. Anything wrong? I can feel the tension through your back.

JORDAN

From the day you turned down Mr. Barrley's ridiculous proposal, Frederick, I knew you had become a man.

FREDERICK

After thirty years.

JORDAN

That's how it is.

FREDERICK

Well. I'm a man. So.

JORDAN

So, seize opportunity. Act on principle and tell rumor to go to hell. You know what I mean.

FREDERICK

Very vaguely . . .
(Pause)
What's all this leading to, Professor?

JORDAN

You know that poem . . .

FREDERICK

What poem . . .

JORDAN

Gray's "Elegy" . . . L-E-G . . . Leg! B-E-G! Beg.

FREDERICK

You've recited it for thirty years . . . I know it backward.

JORDAN

It's really all about obscurity and missed opportunities, you know . . . It's all "perhapses" and "maybes" . . . Listen . . .

FREDERICK

Get to the point, Pop. Don't recite any more.

JORDAN

I'm telling you, boy. The hardest thing for a father is to see his son making his old mistakes. If, when I watch the two of you, I see Albert Perez Jordan and Esther Trout instead of Frederick Jordan and Anna Herschel, then all I would have left you, boy, is my shame and trembling. Since you love the girl, erase history from your mind and make your own. Don't ask her questions and don't let her ask you; take her as she is with what she has, and teach her to accept you the same way. But history, gossip, rumor, and what people go say? Blank it out! You have the strength. From the day you refused to sell that roof for money, I knew you had it.

FREDERICK

I got it from you.

JORDAN

That girl's got qualities you need. She's bright, she's honest; take her, with my blessing.

FREDERICK

That's the trouble with you, Pop. She ain't yours to give away. You don't own the world. Stop getting on like is yours. Is up to her, not you.

JORDAN

I'm sorry. Yes. I see your point. Don't hide in the men's room all your life . . .

FREDERICK

What the hell does that mean?

(*Enter* ANNA)

JORDAN

It means . . . It means I'm going to have a pee!

(*Exits*)

ANNA

What's wrong?

FREDERICK

He says he can't afford to change his glasses, but he's going blind, I think. It makes him irritable.

ANNA

Maybe he's just shortsighted. The first night I came in here, he peered very closely at me and called me another name: Esther. Who was Esther?

FREDERICK

You read the stories. You mean, if she was real?

ANNA

Yeah. If she was, that was an awful thing to do. Stand her up like that.

FREDERICK

Why not? It's just another honky.

76

ANNA

Freddie Jordan, you lousy black chauvinist, come here! Come
here!
  (*She chases him, a mock fight, they embrace*)
Have you told him?

FREDERICK

Not yet.

ANNA

Do you want me to?

FREDERICK

No, Anna. Let me do it.

(JORDAN *returns to the room*)

JORDAN

Oh, sorry. You're talking. I won't interrupt.

ANNA

Please stay, Mr. Jordan . . . Sit. Frederick wants to . . .

JORDAN

I know. I know . . .

FREDERICK

No, you *don't* know. I've been listening to you all my life. Now
it's your turn.

JORDAN

Shall we say I've guessed?

FREDERICK

  (*To* ANNA)
He drives you crazy, you know that? You see what I was saying.

JORDAN

I'm just excited, that's all. I'll be quiet.
(*Pause*)
I'm quiet.
(*Pause*)
Stone still.
(*Pause*)
Dumb as a gravestone.

FREDERICK

Anna's leaving. Wait . . .

ANNA

It's time I left. This is getting to be home, and it isn't. That's
what we were talking about in the little park. I've got my
strength back now, thanks to you and Mrs. Jordan, and I'm
ready to go back. I got the money yesterday, but I couldn't find
the strength to tell you.

JORDAN

You know you can stay as long as you like. The last week has
been . . . Well, I've been very happy. I think you're lucky,
too. You see how it all turns out? Where there's hope, there's
trout. You've got a fine man in Frederick. He's got his old
man's best qualities . . .

FREDERICK

You're rushing things, Dad.

JORDAN

(*Rises excitedly*)
You can bet your backside I rushing things, boy. Excuse me,
but I am rushing things because you see that clock there? Look
at it!

FREDERICK
    Goddamnit, Daddy, listen . . .

ANNA
    Please, Mr. Jordan . . .

JORDAN
    Esther . . .

ANNA
    Anna is my name . . .

JORDAN
    That pendulum is a little ax cutting off a piece of your life
    every time it swings. And I say, Don't hesitate. Do what you
    know you must do, and defy the world.

ANNA
    I wish you'd settle down, Mr. Jordan.

JORDAN
    I'm settled. Anna. Anna Herschel.

ANNA
    I'm going. I said so. And I'm not going with your son. I'm not
    going away with him. We love each other, but not in the way
    you mean. Are you listening?

JORDAN
    I am listening. I've heard it all before . . . But I'm listening.

ANNA
    "I've grown to love it here. You mustn't make fun of that.
    Albert, I think you're a silly, affected, but lovely man. You've

pestered me relentlessly for three months. It's been worse than the Blitz.

(*Projection:* ESTHER *in uniform*)

"And I've thought very carefully about this, all the possible complications, but if you want me to, I'll marry you."

(*Projection fades*)

You weren't listening, Mr. Jordan.

(JORDAN *rises and looks at them vacantly*)

JORDAN

I was listening. I heard it before. When are you going, then?

ANNA

Now. It's easier. Frederick's phoned for a taxi and I'm packed.

FREDERICK

I'm taking her to the airport.

JORDAN

Go on that plane with her, boy! Don't be a damn fool like your old man! From the time that crazy Yankee wanted to buy this roof, you should have gone. You made the one mistake that costs you later! Now you getting a next chance! Leave this place. It dried me up and it will dry you up. You're an artist, boy. You're one of God's chosen. That's what that blasted poem is all about. Don't bury yourself out here. Go on that plane!

(*Pause*)

I'm sorry.

FREDERICK

You stayed here. I'm staying.

(JORDAN *exits*)

ANNA

Doesn't he ever give up? He might have made an exciting father-in-law, though.

FREDERICK

We discussed all that.
(*A taxi horn blows outside*)
The guy's here.

(MABEL *enters*)

MABEL

You know you can stay till you sort yourself out.
(ANNA *controls herself, and then leaves*)
Where is his majesty Montezuma? 'Cause I don't feel so good.

FREDERICK

Outside somewhere sulking, I suppose. That man thinks I must repeat his life. Correct what he didn't do. And I can't reach him. The same damn way Junior couldn't reach him.

MABEL

That man? That man is your father. He taught some of the best people in this country. Don't refer to him as "that man." I don't know why he so desperate.
(ANNA *enters with the baby and a bag*)
Albert! Albert! Come in here, please.

ANNA

I could leave him a note.

MABEL

No. He will come.

ANNA

Well, what can I tell you all? I had a home for one week. I found my strength again just watching you. I don't write letters, but maybe I can put it all down someday. Frederick, you want to help me with this bag? . . . Is he going to come out, you think?

MABEL

Albert!

(JORDAN emerges, carrying a small rose)

JORDAN

I was in the garden, gathering this rose for Pavlova.
(*Recites*)
"Full many a gem of purest ray serene . . ."

MABEL

Oh, God, poetry again . . .

JORDAN

(*Recites*)
"The dark, unfathomed caves of ocean bear . . .
(*The taxi horn hoots*)
Full many a flower is born to blush unseen,
    And waste its sweetness on the desert air . . ."
(*Kisses her*)
They use poppies on Remembrance Day, Miss Hope. But for you, there is this little flower, Miss Esther Anna Herschel Trout.

MABEL

That damn taxi only honking, honking . . .

JORDAN

"Jordan is a honky,
Jordan is a donkey,
Jordan is a . . ."

ANNA

We're about ready to go now.

JORDAN

The taxi reach already?

(*They bring the baby to him*)

MABEL

Say something, nuh, Albert.
(*Pause*)
Albert, the cat got your tongue?

(JORDAN *closes his eyes, holds a hand above the baby in a benediction*)

JORDAN

May this child . . . May this child . . .
(*He hands it to* MABEL)
Here. Take the damn thing.

(*Goes into the next room*)

MABEL

Here.
(*She gives* ANNA *the baby, follows* JORDAN *into the next room*)
What happen to you? What is it that happen, Albert? Is
Junior? Tell me. You could talk to me. What you self crying
like a baby for? Albert, grow up!

(FREDERICK and ANNA *wait*)

FREDERICK

He'll be all right. Come.

ANNA

Goodbye. Goodbye!

(MABEL *enters the room and goes to the window*)

MABEL

Goodbye, Anna. Ba-bye! Ba-bye!
(*She stands there watching, as* JORDAN *enters*)
Lord, I have this pain in me chest, you see. Damn thing killing me.

(*Fade*)

MABEL

I getting ready to go now, Albert. Sit still where you are and don't get up. I getting ready. I have fought the good fight, as the Book says. I have finished my work, and though the good fight was mainly with you, I ent frighten. I have Junior out there, and a whole set of people I ent so keen on meeting, but is not my place who the Lord invite. All I can say is that I only gone ahead to polish the crown He will have for you. 'Cause you was argumentative, stupid, and a stubborn man, but you was a king to me. I tired now, and I going. Turn off the stove. And, Albert . . .
(*She has turned, then turns back*)
Don't bother with the sweepstake ticket, you hear? 'Cause you ent going win it.

(*Exit.* JORDAN *alone*)

JORDAN

My old queen is gone. And Albert, my young prince. Ah, Ezra, Ezra! I armed for death, and was unarmed by loss. I've had a son shot in the Black Power riots. I thought he did it out of contempt for me—not out of hope for others—and it has not changed this country. The other one has chosen a slower death in this place—art. He lives like a hermit up in the country now. I gave them to this country—one for politics and one for art. My brother the railway porter is now head of the local union in Hartford, Connecticut, and keeps begging me halfheartedly to come to the States. He knows damn well I'd be a misfit there. I'd be a misfit in England, too. I've been there once, and I found it a mean place. Remember what we saw, Pilly? An archipelago in a beautiful sea. Cities where all the races joined to make one race. Athens. The glory that was Greece. You remember, man, Pilly. Can't tell me you don't remember . . .

(PILGRIM, *in black, with sash appears on the veranda*)

PILGRIM

I remember. I remember it damn well.

JORDAN

Some educational conference. Every day there I was, frightened I'd bump into Esther Hope. They took us out by train to a farm in the Berkshires, Pilly, chaps from Malta, the Sudan, from all over the Commonwealth. Ceylon . . . In that malicious cold.

PILGRIM

That was the sadness of our generation, A.P. It was like a light going out in our minds, the empire fading. Bought a sweepstake ticket for the first time in my life yesterday.

JORDAN
> You, Pilly?
> (*Laughs*)
> Why?

PILGRIM
> Well, I feel I pushing on myself, Albert. Don't get up. And don't give up. Keep up them remembrances. They going good. I'll send that boy around.

(*He recedes into darkness.* INTERVIEWER *enters as before*)

JORDAN
> I taught those little bastards well, didn't I? I taught with a passion. Wrong things or not. Some of them are big shots today, judges. But I was a holy terror in that classroom, boy, Pilly. There would be a deathly silence when I entered, the kind of silence that we keep for kings. I taught them with the love that comes through books and I inspired the fear that would give them confidence.
> (*He rises*)
> And though I old, Pilly boy! Where you? Don't leave too, Ezra Pilgrim. Though I old, and this hand that used to hold that leather strap like a scepter, quivering, I still say: Let lightning flash from your eye when you remember those dead, all those dead, arranged in your memory, grave after grave, like empty desks in a classroom, knowing that is the old One Jacket Jordan thundering to teach, to teach!
> (*He has put on his jacket. He crosses to the desk. As young* JORDAN)
> I am trying to tell all you blasted young whippersnappers that Thomas Gray is saying: It doesn't matter where you're born, how obscure you are, that fame and fortune are contained within you. Your body is the earth in which it springs and dies. And it's the humble people of this world, you Junes, you

Walcott, and you Brown, and you Fonesca, and you Mango Head, that he's concerned about. And he's concerned about them from the very first verse of his "Elegy" as he meditates aloud. Now, class, close books and recite from memory!

(*He recites each line and the class recites after him*)

JORDAN AND VOICES
    "The curfew tolls the knell of parting day,
        The lowing herd wind slowly o'er the lea
      The ploughman homeward plods his weary way,
        And leaves the world to darkness and to me."

(*Fadeout*)

Pantomime

For Wilbert Holder

Characters

HARRY TREWE, *English, mid-forties, owner of the Castaways Guest House, retired actor*

JACKSON PHILLIP, *Trinidadian, forty, his factotum, retired calypsonian*

The action takes place in a gazebo on the edge of a cliff, part of a guest house on the island of Tobago, West Indies.

Pantomime was first produced by All Theatre Productions at the Little Carib Theatre, Port of Spain, Trinidad, on April 12, 1978, directed by Albert LaVeau, with the following cast:

HARRY TREWE   Maurice Brash
JACKSON PHILLIP   Wilbert Holder

The play was produced by Liane Aukin for the British Broadcasting Corporation on January 25, 1979, with the following cast:

HARRY TREWE   Robert Lang
JACKSON PHILLIP   Norman Beaton

Act One

A small summerhouse or gazebo, painted white, with a few plants and a table set for breakfast. HARRY TREWE enters—in white, carrying a tape recorder, which he rests on the table. He starts the machine.

HARRY

>   (Sings and dances)
> *It's our Christmas panto,*
> *it's called: Robinson Crusoe.*
> *We're awfully glad that you've shown up,*
> *it's for kiddies as well as for grown-ups.*
> *Our purpose is to please:*
> *so now with our magic wand . . .*
>   (Dissatisfied with the routine, he switches off the machine. Rehearses his dance. Then presses the machine again)
> *Just picture a lonely island*
> *and a beach with its golden sand.*
> *There walks a single man*
> *in the beautiful West Indies!*

(*He turns off the machine. Stands, staring out to sea. Then exits with the tape recorder. Stage empty for a few beats, then* JACKSON, *in an open, white waiter's jacket and black trousers, but barefoot, enters with a breakfast tray. He puts the tray down, looks around*)

JACKSON
    Mr. Trewe?
        (*English accent*)
    Mr. Trewe, your scramble eggs is here! *are* here!
        (*Creole accent*)
    You hear, Mr. Trewe? I here wid your eggs!
        (*English accent*)
    Are you in there?
        (*To himself*)
    And when his eggs get cold, is I to catch.
        (*He fans the eggs with one hand*)
    What the hell I doing? That ain't go heat them. It go make them more cold. Well, he must be leap off the ledge. At long last. Well, if he ain't dead, he could call.

(*He exits with tray. Stage bare.* HARRY *returns, carrying a hat made of goatskin and a goatskin parasol. He puts on the hat, shoulders the parasol, and circles the table. Then he recoils, looking down at the floor*)

HARRY
        (*Sings and dances*)
    Is this the footprint of a naked man,
    or is it the naked footprint of a man,
    that startles me this morning on this bright and golden sand.
        (*To audience*)
    There's no one here but I,
    just the sea and lonely sky . . .
        (*Pauses*)
    Yes . . . and how the hell did it go on?

(JACKSON *enters, without the tray. Studies* HARRY)

JACKSON

Morning, Mr. Trewe. Your breakfast ready.

HARRY

So how're you this morning, Jackson?

JACKSON

Oh, fair to fine, with seas moderate, with waves three to four feet in open water, and you, sir?

HARRY

Overcast with sunny periods, with the possibility of heavy showers by mid-afternoon, I'd say, Jackson.

JACKSON

Heavy showers, Mr. Trewe?

HARRY

Heavy showers. I'm so bloody bored I could burst into tears.

JACKSON

I bringing in breakfast.

HARRY

You do that, Friday.

JACKSON

Friday? It ain't go keep.

HARRY

(Gesturing)
Friday, you, bring Crusoe, me, breakfast now. Crusoe hungry.

JACKSON

Mr. Trewe, you come back with that same rake again? I tell
you, I ain't no actor, and I ain't walking in front a set of tourists
naked playing cannibal. Carnival, but not canni-bal.

HARRY

What tourists? We're closed for repairs. We're the only ones
in the guest house. Apart from the carpenter, if he ever
shows up.

JACKSON

Well, you ain't seeing him today, because he was out on a
heavy lime last night . . . Saturday, you know? And with the
peanuts you does pay him for overtime.

HARRY

All right, then. It's goodbye!

(*He climbs onto the ledge between the uprights, teetering, walking
slowly*)

JACKSON

Get offa that ledge, Mr. Trewe! Is a straight drop to them
rocks!

(HARRY *kneels, arms extended, Jolson-style*)

HARRY

Hold on below there, sonny boooy! Daddy's a-coming. Your
papa's a-coming, Sonnnnneee Boooooooy!
    (*To* JACKSON)
You're watching the great Harry Trewe and his high-wire act.

JACKSON

You watching Jackson Phillip and his disappearing act.

(*Turning to leave*)

HARRY

(*Jumping down*)
I'm not a suicide, Jackson. It's a good act, but you never read the reviews. It would be too exasperating, anyway.

JACKSON

What, sir?

HARRY

Attempted suicide in a Third World country. You can't leave a note because the pencils break, you can't cut your wrist with the local blades . . .

JACKSON

We trying we best, sir, since all you gone.

HARRY

Doesn't matter if we're a minority group. Suicides are tax-payers, too, you know, Jackson.

JACKSON

Except it ain't going be suicide. They go say I push you. So, now the fun and dance done, sir, breakfast now?

HARRY

I'm rotting from insomnia, Jackson. I've been up since three, hearing imaginary guests arriving in the rooms, and I haven't slept since. I nearly came around the back to have a little talk. I started thinking about the same bloody problem, which is, What entertainment can we give the guests?

JACKSON

They ain't guests, Mr. Trewe. They's casualties.

HARRY

How do you mean?

JACKSON

This hotel like a hospital. The toilet catch asthma, the air-condition got ague, the front-balcony rail missing four teet', and every minute the fridge like it dancing the Shango . . . brrgudup . . . jukjuk . . . brrugudup. Is no wonder that the carpenter collapse. Termites jumping like steel band in the foundations.

HARRY

For fifty dollars a day they want Acapulco?

JACKSON

Try giving them the basics: Food. Water. Shelter. They ain't shipwrecked, they pay in advance for their vacation.

HARRY

Very funny. But the ad says, "Tours" and "Nightly Entertainment." Well, Christ, after they've seen the molting parrot in the lobby and the faded sea fans, they'll be pretty livid if there's no "nightly entertainment," and so would you, right? So, Mr. Jackson, it's your neck and mine. We open next Friday.

JACKSON

Breakfast, sir. Or else is overtime.

HARRY

I kept thinking about this panto I co-authored, man. *Robinson Crusoe*, and I picked up this old script. I can bring it all down to your level, with just two characters. Crusoe, Man Friday, maybe even the parrot, if that horny old bugger will remember his lines . . .

JACKSON

Since we on the subject, Mr. Trewe, I am compelled to report that parrot again.

HARRY

No, not again, Jackson?

JACKSON

Yes.

HARRY

(*Imitating parrot*)
Heinegger, Heinegger.
(*In his own voice*)
Correct?

JACKSON

Wait, wait! I know your explanation: that a old German called Herr Heinegger used to own this place, and that when that maquereau of a macaw keep cracking: "Heinegger, Heinegger," he remembering the Nazi and not heckling me, but it playing a little havoc with me nerves. This is my fifth report. I am marking them down. Language is ideas, Mr. Trewe. And I think that this pre-colonial parrot have the wrong idea.

HARRY

It's his accent, Jackson. He's a Creole parrot. What can I do?

JACKSON

Well, I am not saying not to give the bird a fair trial, but I see nothing wrong in taking him out the cage at dawn, blindfolding the bitch, giving him a last cigarette if he want it, lining him up against the garden wall, and perforating his arse by firing squad.

HARRY

The war's over, Jackson! And how can a bloody parrot be prejudiced?

JACKSON

The same damn way they corrupt a child. By their upbringing. That parrot survive from a pre-colonial epoch, Mr. Trewe, and if it want to last in Trinidad and Tobago, then it go have to adjust.

(*Long pause*)

HARRY
      (*Leaping up*)
Do you think we could work him into the panto? Give him something to do? Crusoe had a parrot, didn't he? You're right, Jackson, let's drop him from the show.

JACKSON

Mr. Trewe, you are a truly, truly stubborn man. I am *not* putting that old goatskin hat on my head and making an ass of myself for a million dollars, and I have said so already.

HARRY

You got it wrong. I put the hat on, I'm . . . Wait, wait a minute. *Cut! Cut!* You know what would be a heavy twist, heavy with irony?

JACKSON
What, Mr. Trewe?

HARRY

We reverse it.

(Pause)

JACKSON

You mean you prepared to walk round naked as your mother make you, in your jockstrap, playing a white cannibal in front of your own people? You're a real actor! And you got balls, too, excuse me, Mr. Trewe, to even consider doing a thing like that! Good. Joke finish. Breakfast now, eh? Because I ha' to fix the sun deck since the carpenter ain't reach.

HARRY

All right, breakfast. Just heat it a little.

JACKSON

Right, sir. The coffee must be warm still. But I best do some brand-new scramble eggs.

HARRY

Never mind the eggs, then. Slip in some toast, butter, and jam.

JACKSON

How long you in this hotel business, sir? No butter. Marge. No sugar. Big strike. Island-wide shortage. We down to half a bag.

HARRY

Don't forget I've heard you sing calypsos, Jackson. Right back there in the kitchen.

JACKSON

Mr. Trewe, every day I keep begging you to stop trying to make a entertainer out of me. I finish with show business. I finish with Trinidad. I come to Tobago for peace and quiet. I quite satisfy. If you ain't want me to resign, best drop the topic.

(*Exits.* HARRY *sits at the table, staring out to sea. He is reciting softly to himself, then more audibly*)

HARRY

"Alone, alone, all, all alone,
  Alone on a wide wide sea . . .
  I bit my arm, I sucked the blood,
  And cried, A sail! a sail!"
      (*He removes the hat, then his shirt, rolls up his trousers, removes them, puts them back on, removes them again*)
Mastah . . . Mastah . . . Friday sorry. Friday never do it again. Master.

(JACKSON *enters with breakfast tray, groans, turns to leave. Returns*)

JACKSON

Mr. Trewe, what it is going on on this blessed Sunday morning, if I may ask?

HARRY

I was feeling what it was like to be Friday.

JACKSON

Well, Mr. Trewe, you ain't mind putting back on your pants?

HARRY

Why can't I eat breakfast like this?

102

JACKSON

Because I am here. I happen to be here. I am the one serving you, Mr. Trewe.

HARRY

There's nobody here.

JACKSON

Mr. Harry, you putting on back your pants?

HARRY

You're frightened of something?

JACKSON

You putting on back your pants?

HARRY

What're you afraid of? Think I'm bent? That's such a corny interpretation of the Crusoe-Friday relationship, boy. My son's been dead three years, Jackson, and I'vn't had much interest in women since, but I haven't gone queer, either. And to be a flasher, you need an audience.

JACKSON

Mr. Trewe, I am trying to explain that I myself feel like a ass holding this tray in my hand while you standing up there naked, and that if anybody should happen to pass, my name is immediately mud. So, when you put back on your pants, I will serve your breakfast.

HARRY

Actors do this sort of thing. I'm getting into a part.

JACKSON
Don't bother getting into the part, get into the pants. Please.

HARRY
Why? You've got me worried now, Jackson.

JACKSON
(*Exploding*)
Put on your blasted pants, man! You like a blasted child, you know!

(*Silence.* HARRY *puts on his pants*)

HARRY
Shirt, too?
(JACKSON *sucks his teeth*)
There.
(HARRY *puts on his shirt*)
You people are such prudes, you know that? What's it in you, Jackson, that gets so Victorian about a man in his own hotel deciding to have breakfast in his own underwear, on a totally deserted Sunday morning?

JACKSON
Manners, sir. Manners.

(*He puts down the tray*)

HARRY
Sit.

JACKSON
Sit? Sit where? How you mean, sit?

HARRY

Sit, and I'll serve breakfast. You can teach me manners. There's more manners in serving than in being served.

JACKSON

I ain't know what it is eating you this Sunday morning, you hear, Mr. Trewe, but I don't feel you have any right to mama-guy me, because I is a big man with three children, all outside. Now, being served by a white man ain't no big deal for me. It happen to me every day in New York, so it's not going to be any particularly thrilling experience. I would like to get break-fast finish with, wash up, finish my work, and go for my sea bath. Now I have worked here six months and never lost my temper, but it wouldn't take much more for me to fling this whole fucking tray out in that sea and get somebody more to your sexual taste.

HARRY

(Laughs)
Aha!

JACKSON

Not aha, oho!

HARRY

(Drawing out a chair)
Mr. Phillips . . .

JACKSON

Phillip. What?

HARRY

Your reservation.

JACKSON

You want me play this game, eh?

(*He walks around, goes to a corner of the gazebo*)

I'll tell you something, you hear, Mr. Trewe? And listen to me good, good. Once and for all. My sense of humor can stretch so far. Then it does snap. You see that sea out there? You know where I born? I born over there. Trinidad. I was a very serious steel-band man, too. And where I come from is a very serious place. I used to get into some serious trouble. A man keep bugging my arse once. A bad john called Boysie. Indian fellow, want to play nigger. Every day in that panyard he would come making joke with nigger boy this, and so on, and I used to just laugh and tell him stop, but he keep laughing and I keep laughing and he going on and I begging him to stop and two of us laughing, until . . .

(*He turns, goes to the tray, and picks up a fork*)

one day, just out of the blue, I pick up a ice pick and walk over to where he and two fellers was playing card, and I nail that ice pick through his hand to the table, and I laugh, and I walk away.

HARRY

Your table, Mr. Phillip.

(*Silence.* JACKSON *shrugs, sits at the table*)

JACKSON

Okay, then. Until.

HARRY

You know, if you want to exchange war experiences, lad, I could bore you with a couple of mine. Want to hear?

JACKSON

My shift is seven-thirty to one.

(*He folds his arms.* HARRY *offers him a cigarette*)

I don't smoke on duty.

HARRY

We put on a show in the army once. Ground crew. RAF. In
what used to be Palestine. A Christmas panto. Another one.
And yours truly here was the dame. The dame in a panto is
played by a man. Well, I got the part. Wrote the music, the
book, everything, whatever original music there was. *Aladdin
and His Wonderful Vamp.* Very obscene, of course. I was the
Wonderful Vamp. Terrific reaction all around. Thanks to me
music-hall background. Went down great. Well, there was a
party afterward. Then a big sergeant in charge of maintenance
started this very boring business of confusing my genius with
my life. Kept pinching my arse and so on. It got kind of boring
after a while. Well, he was the size of a truck, mate. And there
wasn't much I could do but keep blushing and pretending to
be liking it. But the Wonderful Vamp was waiting outside for
him, the Wonderful Vamp and a wrench this big, and after
that, laddie, it took all of maintenance to put him back again.

JACKSON

That is white-man fighting. Anyway, Mr. Trewe, I feel the fun
finish; I would like, with your permission, to get up now and
fix up the sun deck. 'Cause when rain fall . . .

HARRY

Forget the sun deck. I'd say, Jackson, that we've come closer
to a mutual respect, and that things need not get that hostile.
Sit, and let me explain what I had in mind.

107

JACKSON

    I take it that's an order?

HARRY

    You want it to be an order? Okay, it's an order.

JACKSON

    It didn't sound like no order.

HARRY

    Look, I'm a liberal, Jackson. I've done the whole routine. Al-
dermaston, Suez, Ban the Bomb, Burn the Bra, Pity the Poor
Pakis, et cetera. I've even tried jumping up to the steel band
at Notting Hill Gate, and I'd no idea I'd wind up in this ironic
position of giving orders, but if the new script I've been given
says: HARRY TREWE, HOTEL MANAGER, then I'm going to play
Harry Trewe, Hotel Manager, to the hilt, damnit. So *sit*
down! Please. Oh, goddamnit, *sit . . . down . . .*
    (JACKSON *sits. Nods*)
Good. Relax. Smoke. Have a cup of tepid coffee. I sat up from
about three this morning, working out this whole skit in my
head.
    (*Pause*)
Mind putting that hat on for a second, it will help my point.
Come on. It'll make things clearer.

(*He gives* JACKSON *the goatskin hat.* JACKSON, *after a pause, puts it on*)

JACKSON

    I'll take that cigarette.

(HARRY *hands over a cigarette*)

HARRY

They've seen that stuff, time after time. Limbo, dancing girls, fire-eating . . .

JACKSON

Light.

HARRY

Oh, sorry.

(*He lights* JACKSON's *cigarette*)

JACKSON

I listening.

HARRY

We could turn this little place right here into a little cabaret, with some very witty acts. Build up the right audience. Get an edge on the others. So, I thought, Suppose I get this material down to two people. Me and . . . well, me and somebody else. Robinson Crusoe and Man Friday. We could work up a good satire, you know, on the master-servant—no offense—relationship. Labor-management, white-black, and so on . . . Making some trenchant points about topical things, you know. Add that show to the special dinner for the price of one ticket . . .

JACKSON

You have to have music.

HARRY

Pardon?

JACKSON

A show like that should have music. Just a lot of talk is very boring.

HARRY

Right. But I'd have to have somebody help me, and that's where I thought . . . Want to take the hat off?

JACKSON

It ain't bothering me. When you going make your point?

HARRY

We had that little Carnival contest with the staff and you knocked them out improvising, remember that? You had the bloody guests in stitches . . .

JACKSON

You ain't start to talk money yet, Mr. Harry.

HARRY

Just improvising with the quatro. And not the usual welcome to Port of Spain, I am glad to see you again, but I'll tell you, artist to artist, I recognized a real pro, and this is the point of the hat. I want to make a point about the hotel industry, about manners, conduct, to generally improve relations all around. So, whoever it is, you or whoever, plays Crusoe, and I, or whoever it is, get to play Friday, and imagine first of all the humor and then the impact of that. What you think?

JACKSON

You want my honest, professional opinion?

HARRY

Fire away.

JACKSON
　　I think is shit.

HARRY
　　I've never been in shit in my life, my boy.

JACKSON
　　It sound like shit to me, but I could be wrong.

HARRY
　　You could say things in fun about this place, about the whole
　　Caribbean, that would hurt while people laughed. You get
　　half the gate.

JACKSON
　　Half?

HARRY
　　What do you want?

JACKSON
　　I want you to come to your senses, let me fix the sun deck and
　　get down to the beach for my sea bath. So, I put on this hat, I
　　pick up this parasol, and I walk like a mama-poule up and down
　　this stage and you have a black man playing Robinson Crusoe
　　and then a half-naked, white, fish-belly man playing Friday,
　　and you want to tell me it ain't shit?

HARRY
　　It could be hilarious!

JACKSON
　　Hilarious, Mr. Trewe? Supposing I wasn't a waiter, and in-
　　stead of breakfast I was serving you communion, this Sunday

111

morning on this tropical island, and I turn to you, Friday, to teach you my faith, and I tell you, kneel down and eat this man. Well, kneel, nuh! What you think you would say, eh?

(*Pause*)

You, this white savage?

HARRY

No, that's cannibalism.

JACKSON

Is no more cannibalism than to eat a god. Suppose I make you tell me: For three hundred years I have made you my servant. For three hundred years . . .

HARRY

It's pantomime, Jackson, just keep it light . . . Make them laugh.

JACKSON

Okay.

(*Giggling*)

For three hundred years I served you. Three hundred years I served you breakfast in . . . in my white jacket on a white veranda, boss, bwana, effendi, bacra, sahib . . . in that sun that never set on your empire I was your shadow, I did what you did, boss, bwana, effendi, bacra, sahib . . . that was my pantomime. Every movement you made, your shadow copied

. . .

(*Stops giggling*)

and you smiled at me as a child does smile at his shadow's helpless obedience, boss, bwana, effendi, bacra, sahib, Mr. Crusoe. Now . . .

HARRY
   Now?

(JACKSON's *speech is enacted in a trance-like drone, a zombie*)

JACKSON
   But after a while the child does get frighten of the shadow he
   make. He say to himself, That is too much obedience, I better
   hads stop. But the shadow don't stop, no matter if the child
   stop playing that pantomime, and the shadow does follow the
   child everywhere; when he praying, the shadow pray too, when
   he turn round frighten, the shadow turn round too, when he
   hide under the sheet, the shadow hiding too. He cannot get
   rid of it, no matter what, and that is the power and black
   magic of the shadow, boss, bwana, effendi, bacra, sahib, until
   it is the shadow that start dominating the child, it is the servant that start dominating the master . . .
      (*Laughs maniacally, like The Shadow*)
   and that is the victory of the shadow, boss.
      (*Normally*)
   And that is why all them Pakistani and West Indians in England, all them immigrant Fridays driving all you so crazy. And
   they go keep driving you crazy till you go mad. In that sun that
   never set, they's your shadow, you can't shake them off.

HARRY
   Got really carried away that time, didn't you? It's pantomime,
   Jackson, keep it light. Improvise!

JACKSON
   You mean we making it up as we go along?

HARRY
   Right!

JACKSON

Right! I in dat!
   (*He assumes a stern stance and points stiffly*)
Robinson obey Thursday now. Speak Thursday language.
Obey Thursday gods.

HARRY

Jesus Christ!

JACKSON

   (*Inventing language*)
Amaka nobo sakamaka khaki pants kamaluma Jesus Christ!
Jesus Christ kamalogo!
   (*Pause. Then with a violent gesture*)
Kamalongo kaba!

(*Meaning: Jesus is dead!*)

HARRY

Sure.
   (*Pause. Peers forward. Then speaks to an imaginary projec-
   tionist, while* JACKSON *stands, feet apart, arms folded, frowning,
   in the usual stance of the Noble Savage*)
Now, could you run it with the subtitles, please?
   (*He walks over to* JACKSON, *who remains rigid. Like a movie
   director*)
Let's have another take, Big Chief.
   (*To imaginary camera*)
Roll it. Sound!

(JACKSON *shoves* HARRY *aside and strides to the table. He bangs the
heel of his palm on the tabletop*)

JACKSON

Patamba! Patamba! Yes?

HARRY

You want us to strike the prop? The patamba?
(*To cameraman*)
Cut!

JACKSON

(*To cameraman*)
Rogoongo! Rogoongo!

(*Meaning: Keep it rolling*)

HARRY

Cut!

JACKSON

Rogoongo, damnit!
(*Defiantly, furiously,* JACKSON *moves around, first signaling the camera to follow him, then pointing out the objects which he rechristens, shaking or hitting them violently. Slams table*)
Patamba!
(*Rattles beach chair*)
Backaraka! Backaraka!
(*Holds up cup, points with other hand*)
Banda!
(*Drops cup*)
Banda karan!
(*Puts his arm around* HARRY; *points at him*)
Subu!
(*Faster, pointing*)
Masz!
(*Stamping the floor*)
Zohgoooor!
(*Rests his snoring head on his closed palms*)
Oma! Omaaaa!
(*Kneels, looking skyward. Pauses; eyes closed*)

115

Booora! Booora!
    (*Meaning the world. Silence. He rises*)
Cut!
And dat is what it was like, before you come here with your
table this and cup that.

HARRY

All right. Good audition. You get twenty dollars a day without
dialogue.

JACKSON

But why?

HARRY

You never called anything by the same name twice. What's a
table?

JACKSON

I forget.

HARRY

I remember: patamba!

JACKSON

Patamba?

HARRY

Right. You fake.

JACKSON

That's a breakfast table. *Ogushi.* That's a dressing table.
Amanga ogushi. I remember now.

HARRY

I'll tell you one thing, friend. If you want me to learn your
language, you'd better have a gun.

JACKSON

You best play Crusoe, chief. I surrender. All you win.
(*Points wearily*)
Table. Chair. Cup. Man. Jesus. I accept. I accept. All you win.
Long time.

(*Smiles*)

HARRY

All right, then. Improvise, then. Sing us a song. In your new
language, mate. In English. Go ahead. I challenge you.

JACKSON

You what?
(*Rises, takes up parasol, handling it like a guitar, and strolls
around the front row of the audience*)
(*Sings*)
I want to tell you 'bout Robinson Crusoe.
He tell Friday, when I do so, do so.
Whatever I do, you must do like me.
*He make Friday a Good Friday Bohbolee;** *
That was the first example of slavery,
'Cause I am still Friday and you ain't me.
Now Crusoe he was this Christian and all,
And Friday, his slave, was a cannibal,
But one day things bound to go in reverse,
With Crusoe the slave and Friday the boss.

* A Judas effigy beaten at Easter in Trinidad and Tobago.

117

HARRY

Then comes this part where Crusoe sings to the goat. Little hint of animal husbandry:

(*Kneels, embraces an imaginary goat, to the melody of* "Swanee")
(*Sings*)
Nanny, how I love you,
How I love you,
My dear old nanny . . .

JACKSON

Is a li'l obscene.

HARRY

(*Music-hall style*)
Me wife thought so. Know what I used to tell her? Obscene? Well, better to be obscene than not heard. How's that? Harry Trewe, I'm telling you again, the music hall's loss is calypso's gain.

(*Stops*)

(JACKSON *pauses. Stares upward, muttering to himself.* HARRY *turns.* JACKSON *is signaling in the air with a self-congratulatory smile*)

HARRY

What is it? What've we stopped for?
(JACKSON *hisses for silence from* HARRY, *then returns to his reverie. Miming*)
Are you feeling all right, Jackson?
(JACKSON *walks some distance away from* HARRY. *An imaginary guitar suddenly appears in his hand.* HARRY *circles him. Lifts one eyelid, listens to his heartbeat.* JACKSON *revolves,* HARRY *revolves with him.* JACKSON's *whole body is now silently rocking in rhythm. He is laughing to himself. We hear, very loud, a calypso rhythm*)
Two can play this game, Jackson.

(He strides around in imaginary straw hat, twirling a cane. We hear, very loud, music hall. It stops. HARRY *peers at* JACKSON)

JACKSON

You see what you start?
(*Sings*)
Well, a Limey name Trewe came to Tobago.
He was in show business but he had no show,
so in desperation he turn to me
and said: "Mister Phillip" is the two o' we,
one classical actor, and one Creole . . .

HARRY

Wait! Hold it, hold it, man! Don't waste that. Try and remember it. I'll be right back.

JACKSON

Where you going?

HARRY

Tape. Repeat it, and try and keep it. That's what I meant, you see?

JACKSON

You start to exploit me already?

HARRY

That's right. Memorize it.
(*Exits quickly.* JACKSON *removes his shirt and jacket, rolls up his pants above the knee, clears the breakfast tray to one side of the floor, overturns the table, and sits in it, as if it were a boat, as* HARRY *returns with the machine*)
What's all this? I'm ready to tape. What're you up to?
(JACKSON *sits in the upturned table, rowing calmly, and from time to time surveying the horizon. He looks up toward the sky,*

119

*shielding his face from the glare with one hand; then he gestures
to* HARRY)
What?
(JACKSON *flaps his arms around leisurely, like a large sea bird, in-
dicating that* HARRY *should do the same*)
What? What about the song? You'll forget the bloody song. It
was a fluke.

JACKSON

(*Steps out from the table, crosses to* HARRY, *irritated*)
If I suppose to help you with this stupidness, we will have to
cool it and collaborate a little bit. Now, I was in that boat,
rowing, and I was looking up to the sky to see a storm gathering, and I wanted a big white sea bird beating inland from a
storm. So what's the trouble, Mr. Trewe?

HARRY

Sea bird? What sea bird? I'm not going to play a fekking sea
bird.

JACKSON

Mr. Trewe, I'm only asking you to play a white sea bird because I am supposed to play a black explorer.

HARRY

Well, I don't want to do it. Anyway, that's the silliest acting
I've seen in a long time. And Robinson Crusoe wasn't *rowing*
when he got shipwrecked; he was on a huge boat. I didn't
come here to play a sea bird, I came to tape the song.

JACKSON

Well, then, is either the sea bird or the song. And I don't see
any reason why you have to call my acting silly. We suppose
to improvise.

HARRY

All right, Jackson, all right. After I do this part, I hope you can remember the song. Now you just tell me, before we keep stopping, what I am supposed to do, how many animals I'm supposed to play, and . . . you know, and so on, and so on, and then when we get all that part fixed up, we'll tape the song, all right?

JACKSON

That suits me. Now, the way I see it here: whether Robinson Crusoe was on a big boat or not, the idea is that he got . . .
(Pause)
shipwrecked. So I . . . if I am supposed to play Robinson Crusoe my way, then I will choose the way in which I will get shipwrecked. Now, as Robinson Crusoe is rowing, he looks up and he sees this huge white sea bird, which is making loud sea-bird noises, because a storm is coming. And Robinson Crusoe looks up toward the sky and sees that there is this storm. Then, there is a large wave, and Robinson Crusoe finds himself on the beach.

HARRY

Am I supposed to play the beach? Because that's white . . .

JACKSON

Hilarious! Mr. Trewe. Now look, you know, I am doing *you* a favor. On this beach, right? Then he sees a lot of goats. And, because he is naked and he needs clothes, he kills a goat, he takes off the skin, and he makes this parasol here and this hat, so he doesn't go around naked for everybody to see. Now I *know* that there is nobody there, but there is an audience, so the sooner Robinson Crusoe puts on his clothes, then the better and happier we will all be. I am going to go back in the

boat. I am going to look up toward the sky. You will, *please*,
make the sea-bird noises. I will do the wave, I will crash onto
the sand, you will come down like a goat, I will kill you, take
off your skin, make a parasol *and* a hat, and after that, then I
promise you that I will remember the song. And I will sing it
to the best of my ability.
   (*Pause*)
However shitty that is.

HARRY

   I said "silly." Now listen . . .

JACKSON

   Yes, Mr. Trewe?

HARRY

   Okay, if you're a black explorer . . . Wait a minute . . .
wait a minute. If you're really a white explorer but you're
black, shouldn't I play a black sea bird because I'm white?

JACKSON

   Are you . . . going to extend . . . the limits of prejudice to
include . . . the flora and fauna of this island? I am entering the boat.

(*He is stepping into the upturned table or boat, as* HARRY *halfheartedly
imitates a bird, waving his arms*)

HARRY

   Kekkkk, kekkkk,
   kekkk, kekkkk!
      (*Stops*)
   What's wrong?

JACKSON

What's wrong? Mr. Trewe, that is not a sea gull . . . that is some kind of . . . well, I don't know what it is . . . some kind of *jumbie* bird or something.

(Pause)

I am returning to the boat.

(He carefully enters the boat, expecting an interrupting bird cry from HARRY, but there is none, so he begins to row)

HARRY

Kekk! Kekkk.

(He hangs his arms down. Pause)

Er, Jackson, wait a minute. Hold it a second. Come here a minute.

(JACKSON patiently gets out of the boat, elaborately panto-miming lowering his body into shallow water, releasing his hold on the boat, swimming a little distance toward shore, getting up from the shallows, shaking out his hair and hands, wiping his hands on his trousers, jumping up and down on one foot to un-plug water from his clogged ear, seeing HARRY, then walking wearily, like a man who has swum a tremendous distance, and collapsing at HARRY's feet)

Er, Jackson. This is too humiliating. Now, let's just forget it and please don't continue, or you're fired.

(JACKSON leisurely wipes his face with his hands)

JACKSON

It don't go so, Mr. Trewe. You know me to be a meticulous man. I didn't want to do this job. I didn't even want to work here. You convinced me to work here. I have worked as meticu-lously as I can, until I have been promoted. This morning I had no intention of doing what I am doing now; you have al-ways admired the fact that whatever I begin, I finish. Now, I will accept my resignation, if you want me to, *after* we have

123

finished this thing. But I am not leaving in the middle of a job,
that has never been my policy. So you can sit down, as usual,
and watch me work, but until I have finished this whole business of Robinson Crusoe being in the boat

(*He rises and repeats the pantomime*)

looking at an imaginary sea bird, being shipwrecked, killing a
goat, making this hat *and* this parasol, walking up the beach
and finding a naked footprint, which should take me into
about another ten or twelve minutes, at the most, I will pack
my things and I will leave, and you can play *Robinson Crusoe*
all by yourself. My plans were, after this, to take the table like
this . . .

(*He goes to the table, puts it upright*)

Let me show you: take the table, turn it all around, go under
the table . . .

(*He goes under the table*)

and this would now have become Robinson Crusoe's hut.

(*Emerges from under the table and, without looking at* HARRY,
continues to talk)

Now, you just tell me if you think I am overdoing it, or if you
think it's more or less what we agreed on?

(*Pause*)

Okay? But I am not resigning.

(*Turns to* HARRY *slowly*)

You see, it's your people who introduced us to this culture:
Shakespeare, *Robinson Crusoe*, the classics, and so on, and
when we start getting as good as them, you can't leave halfway.
So, I will continue? Please?

HARRY

No, Jackson. You will *not* continue. You will straighten this
table, put back the tablecloth, take away the breakfast things,
give me back the hat, put your jacket back on, and we will
continue as normal and forget the whole matter. Now, I'm
very serious, I've had enough of this farce. I would like to stop.

JACKSON

May I say what I think, Mr. Trewe? I think it's a matter of prejudice. I think that you cannot believe: one: that I can act, and two: that any black man should play Robinson Crusoe. A little while aback, I came out here quite calmly and normally with the breakfast things and find you almost stark naked, kneeling down, and you told me you were getting into your part. Here am I getting into *my* part and you object. This is the story . . . this is history. This moment that we are now acting here is the history of imperialism; it's nothing less than that. And I don't think that I can—should—concede my getting into a part halfway and abandoning things, just because you, as my superior, give me orders. People become independent. Now, I could go down to that beach by myself with this hat, and I could play Robinson Crusoe, I could play Columbus, I could play Sir Francis Drake, I could play anybody discovering anywhere, but I don't want you to tell me when and where to draw the line!

(Pause)

Or what to discover and when to discover it. All right?

HARRY

Look, I'm sorry to interrupt you again, Jackson, but as I—you know—was watching you, I realized it's much more profound than that; that it could get offensive. We're trying to do something light, just a little pantomime, a little satire, a little picong. But if you take this thing seriously, we might commit Art, which is a kind of crime in this society . . . I mean, there'd be a lot of things there that people . . . well, it would make them think too much, and well, we don't want that . . . we just want a little . . . entertainment.

JACKSON

How do you mean, Mr. Trewe?

HARRY

Well, I mean if you . . . well, I mean. If you did the whole thing in reverse . . . I mean, okay, well, all right . . . you've got this black man . . . no, no . . . all right. You've got this man who is black, Robinson Crusoe, and he discovers this island on which there is this white cannibal, all right?

JACKSON

Yes. That is, after he has killed the goat . . .

HARRY

Yes, I know, I know. After he has killed the goat and made a . . . the hat, the parasol, and all of that . . . and, anyway, he comes across this man called Friday.

JACKSON

How do you know I mightn't choose to call him Thursday? Do I have to copy every . . . I mean, are we improvising?

HARRY

All right, so it's Thursday. He comes across this naked white cannibal called Thursday, you know. And then look at what would happen. He would have to start to . . . well, he'd have to, sorry . . . This cannibal, who is a Christian, would have to start unlearning his Christianity. He would have to be taught . . . I mean . . . he'd have to be taught by this—African . . . that everything was wrong, that what he was doing . . . I mean, for nearly two thousand years . . . was wrong. That his civilization, his culture, his whatever, was . . . *horrible*. Was all . . . wrong. Barbarous, I mean, you know. And Crusoe would then have to teach him things like, you know, about . . . Africa, his gods, patamba, and so on . . . and it would get very, very complicated, and I suppose ultimately it would be very boring, and what we'd have on our hands would be . . . would be a play and not a little pantomime . . .

JACKSON

I'm too ambitious?

HARRY

No, no, the whole thing would have to be reversed; white would become black, you know . . .

JACKSON

(Smiling)
You see, Mr. Trewe, I don't see anything wrong with that, up to now.

HARRY

Well, I do. It's not the sort of thing I want, and I think you'd better clean up, and I'm going inside, and when I come back I'd like this whole place just as it was. I mean, just before everything started.

JACKSON

You mean you'd like it returned to its primal state? Natural? Before Crusoe finds Thursday? But, you see, that is not history. That is not the world.

HARRY

No, no, I don't give an Eskimo's fart about the world, Jackson. I just want this little place here *cleaned up*, and I'd like you to get back to fixing the sun deck. Let's forget the whole matter. Righto. Excuse me.

(*He is leaving.* JACKSON'*s tone will stop him*)

JACKSON

Very well. So I take it you don't want to hear the song, neither?

HARRY

No, no, I'm afraid not. I think really it was a silly idea, it's all my fault, and I'd like things to return to where they were.

JACKSON

The story of the British Empire, Mr. Trewe. However, it is too late. The history of the British Empire.

HARRY

Now, how do you get that?

JACKSON

Well, you come to a place, you find that place as God make it; like Robinson Crusoe, you civilize the natives; they try to do something, you turn around and you say to them: "You are not good enough, let's call the whole thing off, return things to normal, you go back to your position as slave or servant, I will keep mine as master, and we'll forget the whole thing ever happened." Correct? You would like me to accept this.

HARRY

You're really making this very difficult, Jackson. Are you hurt? Have I offended you?

JACKSON

Hurt? No, no, no. I didn't expect any less. I am not hurt.
    (Pause)
I am just . . .

(Pause)

HARRY

You're just what?

JACKSON

I am just ashamed . . . of making such a fool of myself.
(*Pause*)
I expected . . . a little respect. That is all.

HARRY

I respect you . . . I just, I . . .

JACKSON

No. It's perfectly all right.
(HARRY *goes to the table, straightens it*)
I . . . no . . . I'll fix the table myself.
(*He doesn't move*)
I am all right, thank you. Sir.
(HARRY *stops fixing the table*)
(*With the hint of a British accent*)
Thank you very much.

HARRY

(*Sighs*)
I . . . am sorry . . . er . . .

(JACKSON *moves toward the table*)

JACKSON

It's perfectly all right, sir. It's perfectly all . . . right.
(*Almost inaudibly*)
Thank you.
(HARRY *begins to straighten the table again*)
No, thank you very much, don't touch anything.
(JACKSON *is up against the table.* HARRY *continues to straighten the table*)
Don't touch anything . . . Mr. Trewe. Please.
(JACKSON *rests one arm on the table, fist closed. They watch each other for three beats*)
Now that . . . is MY order . . .

(*They watch each other for several beats as the lights fade*)

Act Two

Noon. White glare. HARRY, *with shirt unbuttoned, in a deck chair reading a paperback thriller. Sound of intermittent hammering from stage left, where* JACKSON *is repairing the sun-deck slats.* HARRY *rises, decides he should talk to* JACKSON *about the noise, decides against it, and leans back in the deck chair, eyes closed. Hammering has stopped for a long while.* HARRY *opens his eyes, senses* JACKSON'S *presence, turns suddenly, to see him standing quite close, shirtless, holding a hammer.* HARRY *bolts from his chair.*

JACKSON

You know something, sir? While I was up there nailing the sun deck, I just stay so and start giggling all by myself.

HARRY

Oh, yes? Why?

JACKSON

No, I was remembering a feller, you know . . . ahhh, he went for audition once for a play, you know, and the way he, you know, the way he prop . . . present himself to the people,

said . . . ahmm, "You know, I am an actor, you know. I do all kind of acting, classical acting, *Creole* acting." That's when I laugh, you know?
(*Pause*)
I going back and fix the deck, then.
(*Moves off. Stops, turns*)
The . . . the hammering not disturbing you?

HARRY

No, no, it's fine. You have to do it, right? I mean, you volunteered, the carpenter didn't come, right?

JACKSON

Yes. Creole acting. I wonder what kind o' acting dat is.
(*Spins the hammer in the air and does or does not catch it*)
Yul Brynner. *Magnificent Seven.* Picture, papa! A kind of Western Creole acting. It ain't have no English cowboys, eh, Mr. Harry? Something wrong, boy, something wrong.
(*He exits.* HARRY *lies back in the deck chair, the book on his chest, arms locked behind his head. Silence. Hammering violently resumes*)
(*Off*)
Kekkk, kekkkekk, kekk!
Kekkekk, kekkkekk, ekkek!

(HARRY *rises, moves from the deck chair toward the sun deck*)

HARRY

Jackson! What the hell are you doing? What's that noise?

JACKSON

(*Off; loud*)
I doing like a black sea gull, suh!

HARRY

Well, it's very distracting.

JACKSON
> (Off)
>
> Sorry, sir.
>> (HARRY returns. Sits down on the deck chair. Waits for the hammering. Hammering resumes. Then stops. Silence. Then we hear)
>> (Singing loudly)
>
> *I want to tell you 'bout Robinson Crusoe.*
> *He tell Friday, when I do so, do so.*
> *Whatever I do, you must do like me,*
> *He make Friday a Good Friday Bohbolee*
>> (Spoken)
>
> And the chorus:
>> (Sings)
>
> *Laide-die*
> *Laidie, lay-day, de-day-de-die,*
> *Laidee-doo-day-dee-day-dee-die*
> *Laidee-day-doh-dee-day-dee-die*
>
>
> *Now that was the first example of slavery,*
> *'Cause I am still Friday and you ain't me,*
> *Now Crusoe he was this Christian and all,*
> *Friday, his slave, was a cannibal,*
> *But one day things bound to go in reverse,*
> *With Crusoe the slave and Friday the boss . . .*
> *Caiso, boy! Caiso!*

(HARRY rises, goes toward the sun deck)

HARRY
> Jackson, man! Jesus!

(*He returns to the deck chair, is about to sit*)

JACKSON
>   (*Off*)
>   Two more lash and the sun deck finish, sir!
>   (HARRY *waits*)
>   Stand by . . . here they come . . .
>   First lash . . .
>   (*Sound*)
>   Pow!
>   Second lash:
>   (*Two sounds*)
>   Pataow! Job complete! Lunch, Mr. Trewe? You want your
>   lunch now? Couple sandwich or what?

HARRY
>   (*Shouts without turning*)
>   Just bring a couple beers from the icebox, Jackson. And the
>   Scotch.
>   (*To himself*)
>   What the hell, let's all get drunk.
>   (*To* JACKSON)
>   Bring some beer for yourself, too, Jackson!

JACKSON
>   (*Off*)
>   Thank you, Mr. Robinson . . . Thank you, Mr. Trewe, sir!
>   *Cru-soe, Trewe-so!*
>   (*Faster*)
>   Crusoe-Trusoe, Robinson Trewe-so!

HARRY
>   Jesus, Jackson; cut that out and just bring the bloody beer!

JACKSON
>   (*Off*)
>   Right! A beer for you and a beer for me! Now, what else is it
>   going to be? A sandwich for you, but none for me.

(HARRY *picks up the paperback and opens it, removing a folded sheet of paper. He opens it and is reading it carefully, sometimes lifting his head, closing his eyes, as if remembering its contents, then reading again. He puts it into a pocket quickly as* JACKSON *returns, carrying a tray with two beers, a bottle of Scotch, a pitcher of water, and two glasses.* JACKSON *sets them down on the table*)

I'm here, sir. At your command.

HARRY

Sit down. Forget the sandwiches, I don't want to eat. Let's sit down, man to man, and have a drink. That was the most sarcastic hammering I've ever heard, and I know you were trying to get back at me with all those noises and that Uncle Tom crap. So let's have a drink, man to man, and try and work out what happened this morning, all right?

JACKSON

I've forgotten about this morning, sir.

HARRY

No, no, no, I mean, the rest of the day it's going to bother me, you know?

JACKSON

Well, I'm leaving at half-past one.

HARRY

No, but still . . . Let's . . . Okay. Scotch?

JACKSON

I'll stick to beer, sir, thank you.

(HARRY *pours a Scotch and water,* JACKSON *serves himself a beer. Both are still standing*)

HARRY

Sit over there, please, Mr. Phillip. On the deck chair.
(*JACKSON sits on the deck chair, facing* HARRY)
Cheers?

JACKSON

Cheers. Cheers. Deck chair and all.

(*They toast and drink*)

HARRY

All right. Look, I think you misunderstood me this morning.

JACKSON

Why don't we forget the whole thing, sir? Let me finish this
beer and go for my sea bath, and you can spend the rest of the
day all by yourself.
(*Pause*)
Well. What's wrong? What happen, sir? I said something
wrong just now?

HARRY

This place isn't going to drive me crazy, Jackson. Not if I
have to go mad preventing it. Not physically crazy; but you
just start to think crazy thoughts, you know? At the beginning
it's fine; there's the sea, the palm trees, monarch of all I survey
and so on, all that postcard stuff. And then it just becomes
another back yard. God, is there anything deadlier than Sunday afternoons in the tropics when you can't sleep? The horror
and stillness of the heat, the shining, godforsaken sea, the
bored and boring clouds? Especially in an empty boarding
house. You sit by the stagnant pool counting the dead leaves
drifting to the edge. I daresay the terror of emptiness made
me want to act. I wasn't trying to humiliate you. I meant
nothing by it. Now, I don't usually apologize to people. I

135

don't do things to apologize for. When I do them, I mean them, but, in your case, I'd like to apologize.

JACKSON

Well, if you find here boring, go back home. Do something else, nuh?

HARRY

It's not that simple. It's a little more complicated than that. I mean, everything I own is sunk here, you see? There's a little matter of a brilliant actress who drank too much, and a car crash at Brighton after a panto . . . Well. That's neither here nor there now. Right? But I'm determined to make this place work. I gave up the theater for it.

JACKSON

Why?

HARRY

Why? I wanted to be the best. Well, among other things; oh, well, that's neither here nor there. Flopped at too many things, though. Including classical and Creole acting. I just want to make this place work, you know. And a desperate man'll try anything. Even at the cost of his sanity, maybe. I mean, I'd hate to believe that under everything else I was also prejudiced, as well. I wouldn't have any right here, right?

JACKSON

'Tain't prejudice that bothering you, Mr. Trewe; you ain't no parrot to repeat opinion. No, is loneliness that sucking your soul as dry as the sun suck a crab shell. On a Sunday like this, I does watch you. The whole staff does study you. Walking round restless, staring at the sea. You remembering your wife and your son, not right? You ain't get over that yet?

HARRY

Jackson . . .

JACKSON

Is none of my business. But it really lonely here out of season. Is summer, and your own people gone, but come winter they go flock like sandpipers all down that beach. So you lonely, but I could make you forget all o' that. I could make H. Trewe, Esquire, a brand-new man. You come like a challenge.

HARRY

Think I keep to myself too much?

JACKSON

If! You would get your hair cut by phone. You drive so careful you make your car nervous. If you was in charge of the British Empire, you wouldn'ta lose it, you'da misplace it.

HARRY

I see, Jackson.

JACKSON

But all that could change if you do what I tell you.

HARRY

I don't want a new life, thanks.

JACKSON

Same life. Different man. But that stiff upper lip goin' have to quiver a little.

HARRY

What's all this? Obeah? "That old black magic"?

JACKSON

Nothing. I could have the next beer?

HARRY

Go ahead. I'm drinking Scotch.

(JACKSON *takes the other beer, swallows deep, smacks his lips, grins at* HARRY)

JACKSON

Nothing. We will have to continue from where we stop this morning. You will have to be Thursday.

HARRY

Aha, you bastard! It's a thrill giving orders, hey? But I'm not going through all that rubbish again.

JACKSON

All right. Stay as you want. But if you say yes, it go have to be man to man, and none of this boss-and-Jackson business, you see, Trewe . . . I mean, I just call you plain Trewe, for example, and I notice that give you a slight shock. Just a little twitch of the lip, but a shock all the same, eh, Trewe? You see? You twitch again. It would be just me and you, all right? You see, two of we both acting a role here we ain't really really believe in, you know. I ent think you strong enough to give people orders, and I *know* I ain't the kind who like taking *them*. So both of we doesn't have to *improvise* so much as *exaggerate*. We faking, faking all the time. But, man to man, I mean . . .
     (Pause)
that could be something else. Right, Mr. Trewe?

HARRY

Aren't we man to man now?

JACKSON

No, no. We having one of them "playing man-to-man" talks,
where a feller does look a next feller in the eye and say, "Le'
we settle this thing, man to man," and this time the feller who
smiling and saying it, his whole honest intention is to take that
feller by the crotch and rip out he stones, and dig out he eye
and leave him for corbeaux to pick.

(*Silence*)

HARRY

You know, that thing this morning had an effect on me, man
to man now. I didn't think so much about the comedy of
Robinson Crusoe, I thought what we were getting into was a
little sad. So, when I went back to the room, I tried to rest
before lunch, before you began all that vindictive hammering . . .

JACKSON

Vindictive?

HARRY

Man to man: that vindictive hammering and singing, and I
thought, Well, maybe we could do it straight. Make a real
straight thing out of it.

JACKSON

You mean like a tradegy. With one joke?

HARRY

Or a codemy, with none. You mispronounce words on pur-
pose, don't you, Jackson?

(JACKSON *smiles*)

Don't think for one second that I'm not up on your game, Jackson. You're playing the stage nigger with me. I'm an actor, you know. It's a smile in front and a dagger behind your back, right? Or the smile itself is the bloody dagger. I'm aware, chum. I'm aware.

JACKSON

The smile kinda rusty, sir, but it goes with the job. Just like the water in this hotel:
(*Demonstrates*)
I turn it on at seven and lock it off at one.

HARRY

Didn't hire you for the smile; I hired you for your voice. We've the same background. Old-time calypso, old-fashioned music hall:
(*Sings*)
Oh, me wife can't cook and she looks like a horse
And the way she makes coffee is grounds for divorce . . .
(*Does a few steps*)
But when love is at stake she's my Worcester sauce . . .
(*Stops*)
Used to wow them with that. All me own work. Ah, the lost glories of the old music hall, the old provincials, grimy brocade, the old stars faded one by one. The brassy pantomimes! Come from an old music-hall family, you know, Jackson. Me mum had this place she ran for broken-down actors. Had tea with the greats as a tot.
(*Sings softly, hums*)
Oh, me wife can't cook . . .
(*Silence*)
You married, Jackson?

JACKSON

I not too sure, sir.

HARRY

You're not sure?

JACKSON

That's what I said.

HARRY

I know what you mean. I wasn't sure I was when I was. My wife's remarried.

JACKSON

You showed me her photo. And the little boy own.

HARRY

But I'm not. Married. So there's absolutely no hearth for Crusoe to go home to. While you were up there, I rehearsed this thing.
  (*Presents a folded piece of paper*)
Want to read it?

JACKSON

What . . . er . . . what is it . . . a poetry?

HARRY

No, no, not a poetry. A thing I wrote. Just a speech in the play . . . that if . . .

JACKSON

Oho, we back in the play again?

HARRY

Almost. You want to read it?

(*He offers the paper*)

JACKSON

All right.

HARRY

I thought—no offense, now. Man to man. If you were doing
Robinson Crusoe, this is what you'd read.

JACKSON

You want me to read this, right?

HARRY

Yeah.

JACKSON

(Reads slowly)
"O silent sea, O wondrous sunset that I've gazed on ten
thousand times, who will rescue me from this complete deso-
lation? . . . "
(Breaking)
All o' this?

HARRY

If you don't mind. Don't act it. Just read it.
(JACKSON looks at him)
No offense.

JACKSON

(Reads)
"Yes, this is paradise, I know. For I see around me the splendors of nature . . . "

HARRY

Don't act it . . .

JACKSON
>   (*Pauses; then continues*)
>   "How I'd like to fuflee this desolate rock."
>   (*Pauses*)
>   Fuflee? Pardon, but what is a fuflee, Mr. Trewe?

HARRY
>   A fuflee? I've got "fuflee" written there?

JACKSON
>   (*Extends paper, points at word*)
>   So, how you does fuflee, Mr. Harry? Is Anglo-Saxon English?

(HARRY *kneels down and peers at the word. He rises*)

HARRY
>   It's F . . . then F-L-E-E—flee to express his hesitation. It's
>   my own note as an actor. He quivers, he hesitates . . .

JACKSON
>   He quivers, he hesitates, but he still can't fuflee?

HARRY
>   Just leave that line out, Jackson.

JACKSON
>   I like it.

HARRY
>   *Leave it out!*

JACKSON
>   No fuflee?

HARRY
>   I said no.

JACKSON

Just because I read it wrong. I know the word "flee," you know. Like to take off. Flee. Faster than run. Is the extra *F* you put in there so close to flee that had me saying fuflee like a damn ass, but le' we leave it in, nuh? One fuflee ain't go kill anybody. Much less bite them.

(*Silence*)

Get it?

HARRY

Don't take this personally . . .

JACKSON

No fuflees on old Crusoe, boy . . .

HARRY

But, if you're going to do professional theater, Jackson, don't take this personally, more discipline is required. All right?

JACKSON

You write it. Why you don't read it?

HARRY

I wanted to hear it. Okay, give it back . . .

JACKSON

(*Loudly, defiantly*)

"The ferns, the palms like silent sentinels, the wide and silent lagoons that briefly hold my passing, solitary reflection. The volcano . . . "

(*Stops*)

"The volcano." What?

HARRY

. . . "wreathed" . . .

JACKSON

> Oho, oho . . . like a wreath? "The volcano *wreathed* in mist.
> But what is paradise without a woman? Adam in paradise!"

HARRY

> Go ahead.

JACKSON

> (*Restrained*)
> "Adam in paradise had his woman to share his loneliness, but
> I miss the voice of even one consoling creature, the touch of a
> hand, the look of kind eyes. Where is the wife from whom I
> vowed never to be sundered? How old is my little son? If he
> could see his father like this, mad with memories of them . . .
> Even Job had his family. But I am alone, alone, I am all
> alone."
> (*Pause*)
> Oho. You write this?

HARRY

> Yeah.

JACKSON

> Is good. Very good.

HARRY

> Thank you.

JACKSON

> Touching. Very sad. But something missing.

HARRY

> What?

JACKSON

Goats. You leave out the goats.

HARRY

The goats. So what? What've you got with goats, anyway?

JACKSON

Very funny. Very funny, sir.

HARRY

Try calling me Trewe.

JACKSON

Not yet. That will come. Stick to the point. You ask for my opinion and I *gave* you my opinion. No doubt I don't have the brains. But *my* point is that this man ain't facing reality. *There are goats* all around him.

HARRY

You're full of shit.

JACKSON

The man is not facing reality. He is not a practical man *ship-wrecked*.

HARRY

I suppose that's the difference between classical and Creole acting?

(*He pours a drink and downs it furiously*)

JACKSON

If he is not practical, he is not Robinson Crusoe. And yes, is Creole acting, yes. Because years afterward his little son could

look at the parasol and the hat and look at a picture of Daddy
and boast: "My daddy smart, boy. He get shipwreck and first
thing he do is he build a hut, then he kill a goat or two and
make clothes, a parasol and a hat." That way Crusoe *achieve*
something, and his son could boast . . .

HARRY

Only his son is dead.

JACKSON

Whose son dead?

HARRY

Crusoe's.

JACKSON

No, pardner. *Your* son dead. Crusoe wife and child waiting
for him, and he is a practical man and he know somebody go
come and save him . . .

HARRY

(*Almost inaudibly*)
"I bit my arm, I sucked the blood,
  And cried, 'A sail! a sail!' "
How the hell does he know "somebody go come and save him"?
That's shit. That's not in his character at that moment. How
the hell can he know? You're a cruel bastard . . .

JACKSON

(*Enraged*)
Because, you fucking ass, he has faith!

HARRY

(*Laughing*)
Faith? What faith?

147

JACKSON

He not sitting on his shipwrecked arse bawling out . . . what it is you have here?

(Reads)

"O . . ." Where is it?

(Reads)

"O silent sea, O wondrous sunset," and all that shit. No. He shipwrecked. He desperate, he hungry. He look up and he see this fucking goat with its fucking beard watching him and smiling, this goat with its forked fucking beard and square yellow eye just like the fucking devil, standing up there . . .

(Pantomimes the goat and Crusoe in turn)

smiling at him, and putting out its tongue and letting go one fucking *bleeeeeh!* And Robbie ent thinking 'bout his wife and son and O silent sea and O wondrous sunset; no, Robbie is the First True Creole, so he watching the goat with his eyes narrow, narrow, and he say: *blehhh*, eh? You muther-fucker, I go show you *blehhh* in your goat-ass, and vam, vam, next thing is Robbie and the goat, *mano a mano*, man to man, man to goat, goat to man, wrestling on the sand, and next thing we know we hearing one last faint, feeble *bleeeeeeehhhhhhhhhhhhhh*, and Robbie is next seen walking up the beach with a goatskin hat and a goatskin umbrella, feeling like a million dollars because *he have faith!*

HARRY

(Applauds)

Bravo! You're the Christian. I am the cannibal. Bravo!

JACKSON

If I does hammer sarcastic, you does clap sarcastic. Now I want to pee.

HARRY

I think I'll join you.

JACKSON

So because I go and pee, you must pee, too?

HARRY

Subliminal suggestion.

JACKSON

Monkey see, monkey do.

HARRY

You're the bloody ape, mate. You people just came down from the trees.

JACKSON

Say that again, please.

HARRY

I'm going to keep that line.

JACKSON

Oho! Rehearse you rehearsing? I thought you was serious.

HARRY

You go have your pee. I'll run over my monologue.

JACKSON

No, you best do it now, sir. Or it going to be on my mind while we rehearsing that what you really want to do is take a break and pee. We best go together, then.

HARRY

We'll call it the pee break. Off we go, then. How long will you be, then? You people take forever.

JACKSON

Maybe you should hold up a sign, sir, or give some sort of signal when you serious or when you joking, so I can know not to react. I would say five minutes.

HARRY

Five minutes? What is this, my friend, Niagara Falls?

JACKSON

It will take me . . . look, you want me to time it? I treat it like a ritual, I don't just pee for peeing's sake. It will take me about forty to fifty seconds to walk to the servants' toilets . . .

HARRY

Wait a second . . .

JACKSON

No, you wait, please, sir. That's almost one minute, take another fifty seconds to walk back, or even more, because after a good pee a man does be in a mood, both ruminative and grateful that the earth has received his libation, so that makes . . .

HARRY

Hold on, please.

JACKSON

(*Voice rising*)

Jesus, sir, give me a break, nuh? That is almost two minutes, and in between those two minutes it have such solemn and ruminative behavior as opening the fly, looking upward or downward, the ease and relief, the tender shaking, the solemn tucking in, like you putting a little baby back to sleep, the reverse zipping or buttoning, depending on the pants, then, with

the self-congratulating washing of the hands, looking at yourself for at least half a minute in the mirror, then the drying
of hands as if you were a master surgeon just finish a major
operation, and the walk back . . .

HARRY

You said that. Any way you look at it, it's under five minutes,
and I interrupted you because . . .

JACKSON

I could go and you could time me, to see if I on a go-slow,
or wasting up my employer's precious time, but I know it will
take at least five, unless, like most white people, you either
don't flush it, a part I forgot, or just wipe your hands fast fast
or not at all . . .

HARRY

Which white people, Jackson?

JACKSON

I was bathroom attendant at the Hilton, and I know men
and races from their urinary habits, and most Englishmen . . .

HARRY

Most Englishmen . . . Look, I was trying to tell you, instead
of going all the way round to the servants' lavatories, pop into
my place, have a quick one, and that'll be under five bloody
minutes in any circumstances and regardless of the capacity.
Go on. I'm all right.

JACKSON
Use your bathroom, Mr. Harry?

HARRY
Go on, will you?

JACKSON

I want to get this. You giving me permission to go through your living room, with all your valuables lying about, with the picture of your wife watching me in case I should leave the bathroom open, and you are granting me the privilege of taking out my thing, doing my thing right there among all those lotions and expensive soaps, and . . . after I finish, wiping my hands on a clean towel?

HARRY

Since you make it so vividly horrible, why don't you just walk around to the servants' quarters and take as much time as you like? Five minutes won't kill me.

JACKSON

I mean, equality is equality and art is art, Mr. Harry, but to use those clean, rough Cannon towels . . . You mustn't rush things, people have to slide into independence. They give these islands independence so fast that people still ain't recover from the shock, so they pissing and wiping their hands indiscriminately. You don't want that to happen in this guest house, Mr. Harry. Let me take my little five minutes, as usual, and if you have to go, you go to your place, and I'll go to mine, and let's keep things that way until I can feel I can use your towels without a profound sense of gratitude, and you could, if you wanted, a little later maybe, walk round the guest house in the dark, put your foot in the squelch of those who missed the pit by the outhouse, that charming old-fashioned outhouse so many tourists take Polaroids of, without feeling degraded, and we can then respect each other as artists. So, I appreciate the offer, but I'll be back in five. Kindly excuse me.

(*He exits*)

HARRY

You've got logorrhea, Jackson. You've been running your mouth like a parrot's arse. But don't get sarcastic with me, boy!

(JACKSON *returns*)

JACKSON

You don't understand, Mr. Harry. My problem is, I really mean what I say.

HARRY

You've been pretending indifference to this game, Jackson, but you've manipulated it your way, haven't you? Now you can spew out all that bitterness in fun, can't you? Well, we'd better get things straight around here, friend. You're still on duty. And if you stay out there too long, your job is at stake. It's . . .
(*Consulting his watch*)
five minutes to one now. You've got exactly three minutes to get in there and back, and two minutes left to finish straightening this place. It's a bloody mess.

(*Silence*)

JACKSON

Bloody mess, eh?

HARRY

That's correct.

JACKSON

(*In exaggerated British accent*)
I go try and make it back in five, bwana. If I don't, the mess could be bloodier. I saw a sign once in a lavatory in Mobile,

Alabama. COLORED. But it didn't have no time limit. Funny, eh?

HARRY

Ape! Mimic! Three bloody minutes!

(JACKSON *exits, shaking his head.* HARRY *recovers the sheet of paper from the floor and puts it back in his pants pocket. He pours a large drink, swallows it all in two large gulps, then puts the glass down. He looks around the gazebo, wipes his hands briskly. He removes the drinks tray with Scotch, the two beer bottles, glasses, water pitcher, and sets them in a corner of the gazebo. He lifts up the deck chair and sets it, sideways, in another corner. He turns the table carefully over on its side; then, when it is on its back, he looks at it. He changes his mind and carefully tilts the table back upright. He removes his shirt and folds it and places it in another corner of the gazebo. He rolls up his trouser cuffs almost to the knee. He is now half-naked. He goes over to the drinks tray and pours the bowl of melted ice, now tepid water, over his head. He ruffles his hair, his face dripping; then he sees an ice pick. He picks it up*)

JACKSON'S VOICE

"One day, just out of the blue, I pick up a ice pick and walk over to where he and two fellers was playing cards, and I nail that ice pick through his hand to the table, and I laugh . . ."

(HARRY *drives the ice pick hard into the tabletop, steps back, looking at it. Then he moves up to it, wrenches it out, and gets under the table, the ice pick at his feet. A few beats, then* JACKSON *enters, pauses*)

JACKSON

(Laughs)
What you doing under the table, Mr. Trewe?
(Silence. JACKSON *steps nearer the table*)
Trewe? You all right?
(Silence. JACKSON *crouches close to* HARRY)
Harry, boy, you cool?

(JACKSON *rises. Moves away some distance. He takes in the* *space. An arena. Then he crouches again*)

Ice-pick time, then?

Okay. "Fee fi fo fum,

I smell the blood of an Englishman . . ."

(JACKSON *exits quickly.* HARRY *waits a while, then crawls from* *under the table, straightens up, and places the ice pick gently* *on the tabletop. He goes to the drinks tray and has a sip from* *the Scotch; then replaces the bottle and takes up a position be-* *hind the table.* JACKSON *returns dressed as Crusoe—goatskin* *hat, open umbrella, the hammer stuck in the waistband of his* *rolled-up trousers. He throws something across the room to* HARRY's *feet. The dead parrot, in a carry-away box.* HARRY *opens it*)

One parrot, to go! Or you eating it here?

HARRY

You son of a bitch.

JACKSON

Sure.

(HARRY *picks up the parrot and hurls it into the sea*)

First bath in five years.

(JACKSON *moves toward the table, very calmly*)

HARRY

You're a bloody savage. Why'd you strangle him?

JACKSON

(*As Friday*)

Me na strangle him, bwana. Him choke from prejudice.

HARRY

Prejudice? A bloody parrot. The bloody thing can't reason.

(*Pause. They stare at each other.* HARRY *crouches, tilts his head,* *shifts on his perch, flutters his wings like the parrot, squawks*)

155

Heinegger. Heinegger.

(JACKSON *stands over the table and folds the umbrella*)

You people create nothing. You imitate everything. It's all been done before, you see, Jackson. The parrot. Think that's something? It's from *The Seagull*. It's from *Miss Julie*. You can't ever be original, boy. That's the trouble with shadows, right? They can't think for themselves.

(JACKSON *shrugs, looking away from him*)

So you take it out on a parrot. Is that one of your African sacrifices, eh?

JACKSON

Run your mouth, Harry, run your mouth.

HARRY

(*Squawks*)

Heinegger . . . Heinegger . . .

(JACKSON *folds the parasol and moves to enter the upturned table*)

I wouldn't go under there if I were you, Jackson.

(JACKSON *reaches into the back of his waistband and removes a hammer*)

JACKSON

The first English cowboy.

(*He turns and faces* HARRY)

HARRY

It's my property. Don't get in there.

JACKSON

The hut. That was my idea.

HARRY
   The table's mine.

JACKSON
   What else is yours, Harry?
      (*Gestures*)
   This whole fucking island? Dem days gone, boy.

HARRY
   The costume's mine, too.
      (*He crosses over, almost nudging* JACKSON, *and picks up the ice
      pick*)
   I'd like them back.

JACKSON
   Suit yourself.

(HARRY *crosses to the other side, sits on the edge of the wall or leans
against a post.* JACKSON *removes the hat and throws it into the arena,
then the parasol*)

HARRY
   The hammer's mine.

JACKSON
   I feel I go need it.

HARRY
   If you keep it, you're a bloody thief.

(JACKSON *suddenly drops to the floor on his knees, letting go of the
hammer, weeping and cringing, and advancing on his knees toward
*HARRY)

157

JACKSON

Pardon, master, pardon! Friday bad boy! Friday wicked nigger. Sorry. Friday nah t'ief again. Mercy, master. Mercy.
(*He rolls around on the floor, laughing*)
Oh, Jesus, I go dead! I go dead. Ay-ay.

(*Silence.* JACKSON *on the floor, gasping, lying on his back.* HARRY *crosses over, picks up the parasol, opens it, after a little difficulty, then puts on the goatskin hat.* JACKSON *lies on the floor, silent*)

HARRY

I never hit any goddamned maintenance sergeant on the head in the service. I've never hit anybody in my life. Violence makes me sick. I don't believe in ownership. If I'd been more possessive, more authoritative, I don't think she'd have left me. I don't think you ever drove an ice pick through anybody's hand, either. That was just the two of us acting.

JACKSON

Creole acting?
(*He is still lying on the floor*)
Don't be too sure about the ice pick.

HARRY

I'm sure. You're a fake. You're a kind man and you think you have to hide it. A lot of other people could have used that to their own advantage. That's the difference between master and servant.

JACKSON

That master-and-servant shit finish. Bring a beer for me.

(*He is still on his back*)

HARRY

There's no more beer. You want a sip of Scotch?

JACKSON

Anything.

(HARRY *goes to the Scotch, brings over the bottle, stands over* JACK-
SON)

HARRY

Here. To me bloody wife!
    (JACKSON *sits up, begins to move off*)
What's wrong, you forget to flush it?

JACKSON

I don't think you should bad-talk her behind her back.

(*He exits*)

HARRY

Behind her back? She's in England. She's a star. Star? She's
a bloody planet.

(JACKSON *returns, holding the photograph of* HARRY'*s wife*)

JACKSON

If you going bad-talk, I think she should hear what you going
to say, you don't think so, darling?
    (*Addressing the photograph, which he puts down*)
If you have to tell somebody something, tell them to their face.
    (*Addressing the photograph*)
Now, you know all you women, eh? Let the man talk his talk
and don't interrupt.

HARRY

You're fucking bonkers, you know that? Before I hired you, I should have asked for a medical report.

JACKSON

Please tell your ex-wife good afternoon or something. The dame in the pantomime is always played by a man, right?

HARRY

Bullshit.

(JACKSON *sits close to the photograph, wiggling as he ventriloquizes*)

JACKSON

(*In an Englishwoman's voice*)
Is not bullshit at all, Harold. Everything I say you always saying bullshit, bullshit. How can we conduct a civilized conversation if you don't give me a chance? What have I done, Harold, oh, Harold, for you to treat me so?

HARRY

Because you're a silly selfish bitch and you *killed our son!*

JACKSON

(*Crying*)
There, there, you see . . . ?
(*He wipes the eyes of the photograph*)
You're calling me names, it wasn't my fault, and you're calling me names. Can't you ever forgive me for that, Harold?

HARRY

Ha! You never told him that, did you? You neglected to mention that little matter, didn't you, love?

JACKSON

> (*Weeping*)

I love you, Harold. I love you, and I loved him, too. Forgive
me, O God, please, please forgive me . . .

> (*As himself*)

So how it happen? Murder? A accident?

HARRY

> (*To the photograph*)

Love me? You loved me so much you get drunk and you . . .
ah, ah, what's the use? What's the bloody use?

(*Wipes his eyes. Pause*)

JACKSON

> (*As wife*)

I'm crying too, Harold. Let bygones be bygones . . .

> (HARRY *lunges for the photograph, but* JACKSON *whips it away*)
> (*As himself*)

You miss, Harold.

> (*Pause; as wife*)

Harold . . .

> (*Silence*)

Harold . . . speak to me . . . please.

> (*Silence*)

What do you plan to do next?

> (*Sniffs*)

What'll you do now?

HARRY

What difference does it make? . . . All right. I'll tell you
what I'm going to do next, Ellen: you're such a big star, you're
such a luminary, I'm going to leave you to shine by yourself.
I'm giving up this bloody rat race and I'm going to take up
Mike's offer. I'm leaving "the theatuh," which destroyed my

confidence, screwed up my marriage, and made you a star. I'm going somewhere where I can get pissed every day and watch the sun set, like Robinson bloody Crusoe. That's what I'm going to bloody do. You always said it's the only part I could play.

JACKSON

> (As wife)
> Take me with you, then. Let's get away together. I always wanted to see the tropics, the palm trees, the lagoons . . .

(HARRY grabs the photograph from JACKSON; he picks up the ice pick and puts the photograph on the table, pressing it down with one palm)

HARRY

> All right, Ellen, I'm going to . . . You can scream all you like, but I'm going to . . .

(He raises the ice pick)

JACKSON

> (As wife)
> My face is my fortune.

(He sneaks up behind HARRY, whips the photograph away while HARRY is poised with the ice pick)

HARRY

> Your face is your fortune, eh? I'll kill her, Jackson, I'll maim that smirking bitch . . .

(He lunges toward JACKSON, who leaps away, holding the photograph before his face, and runs around the gazebo, shrieking)

JACKSON
>(As wife)

Help! Help! British police! My husband trying to kill me!
Help, somebody, help!
>(HARRY chases JACKSON with the ice pick, but JACKSON nimbly
>avoids him)
>(As wife)
Harry! Have you gone mad?

(He scrambles onto the ledge of the gazebo. He no longer holds the
photograph to his face, but his voice is the wife's)

HARRY

Get down off there, you melodramatic bitch. You're too
bloody conceited to kill yourself. Get down from there, Ellen!
Ellen, it's a straight drop to the sea!

JACKSON
>(As wife)

Push me, then! Push me, Harry! You hate me so much, why
you don't come and push me?

HARRY

Push yourself, then. You never needed my help. Jump!

JACKSON
>(As wife)

Will you forgive me now, or after I jump?

HARRY

Forgive you? . . .

JACKSON
>(As wife)

All right, then. Goodbye!

(He turns, teetering, about to jump)

HARRY
> (*Shouts*)
> *Ellen! Stop! I forgive you!*
>> (JACKSON *turns on the ledge. Silence.* HARRY *is now sitting on the floor*)
>
> That's the real reason I wanted to do the panto. To do it better than you ever did. You played Crusoe in the panto, Ellen. I was Friday. Black bloody greasepaint that made you howl. You wiped the stage with me . . . Ellen . . . well. Why not? I was no bloody good.

JACKSON
> (*As himself*)
> Come back to the play, Mr. Trewe. Is Jackson. We was playing Robinson Crusoe, remember?
> (*Silence*)
> Master, Friday here . . .
> (*Silence*)
> You finish with the play? The panto? Crusoe must get up, he must make himself get up. He have to face a next day again.
> (*Shouts*)
> *I tell you: man must live!* Then, after many years, he see this naked footprint that is the mark of his salvation . . .

HARRY
> (*Recites*)
> "The self-same moment I could pray;
> and . . . tata tee-tum-tum
> The Albatross fell off and sank
> Like lead into the sea."
> God, my memory . . .

JACKSON
> That ain't Crusoe, that is "The Rime of the Ancient Mariner."

(*He pronounces it "Marina"*)

HARRY
Mariner.

JACKSON
Marina.

HARRY
Mariner.

JACKSON
"The Rime of the Ancient Marina." So I learn it in Fourth
Standard.

HARRY
It's your country, mate.

JACKSON
Is your language, pardner. I stand corrected. Now, you ain't see
English crazy? I could sit down right next to you and tell you
I *stand* corrected.

HARRY
Sorry. Where were we, Mr. Phillip?

JACKSON
Tobago. Where are you? It was your cue, Mr. Trewe.

HARRY
Where was I, then?

JACKSON
Ahhhm . . . That speech you was reading . . . that speech . . .

HARRY
Speech?

JACKSON

"O silent sea and so on . . . wreathed in mist . . ." Shall we
take it from there, then? The paper.

HARRY

I should know it. After all, I wrote it. But prompt . . .
   (HARRY *gives* JACKSON *his copy of the paper, rises, walks around,
   looks toward the sea*)
Creole or classical?

JACKSON

Don't make joke.

(*Silence. Sea-gull cries*)

HARRY

Then Crusoe, in his desolation, looks out to the sea, for the
ten thousandth time, and remembers England, his wife, his
little son, and speaks to himself:
   (*As Crusoe*)
"O silent sea, O wondrous sunset that I've gazed on ten
thousand times, who will rescue me from this complete desolation? Yes, this is paradise, I know. For I see around me the
splendors of nature. The ferns, the palms like silent sentinels,
the wide and silent lagoons that briefly hold my passing, solitary reflection. The volcano wreathed in mist. But what is
paradise without a woman? Adam in paradise had his woman
to share his loneliness . . . loneliness . . .

JACKSON

   (*Prompts*)
. . . but I miss the voice . . .

HARRY
(*Remembering*)
"But I miss the voice . . .
(*Weeping, but speaking clearly*)
of even one consoling creature, the touch . . . of a hand . . .
the look of kind eyes . . . Where is the wife from whom I
vowed . . . never to be sundered? How old is my little son?
If he could see his father like this . . . dressed in goatskins
and mad with memories of them?"

(*He breaks down, quietly sobbing. A long pause*)

JACKSON
You crying or you acting?

HARRY
Acting.

JACKSON
I think you crying. Nobody could act that good.

HARRY
How would you know? You an actor?

JACKSON
Maybe not. But I cry a'ready.

HARRY
Okay, I was crying.

JACKSON
For what?

HARRY

> (*Laughs*)
> For what? I got carried away. I'm okay now.

JACKSON

> But you laughing now.

HARRY

> It's the same sound. You can't tell the difference if I turn my
> back.

JACKSON

> Don't make joke.

HARRY

> It's an old actor's trick. I'm going to cry now, all right?

(*He turns, then sobs with laughter, covering and uncovering his face
with his hands.* JACKSON *stalks around, peers at him, then begins to
giggle. They are now both laughing*)

JACKSON

> (*Through laughter*)
> So . . . so . . . next Friday . . . when the tourists come . . .
> Crusoe . . . Crusoe go be ready for them . . . Goat race . . .

HARRY

> (*Laughing*)
> Goat-roti!

JACKSON

> (*Laughing*)
> Gambling.

HARRY

> (*Baffled*)
> Gambling?

JACKSON

> Goat-to-pack. Every night . . .

HARRY

> (*Laughing*)
> Before they goat-to-bed!

JACKSON

> (*Laughing*)
> So he striding up the beach with his little goat-ee . . .

HARRY

> (*Laughing*)
> E-goat-istical, again.

(*Pause*)

JACKSON

> You get the idea. So, you okay, Mr. Trewe?

HARRY

> I'm fine, Mr. Phillip. You know . . .
> (*He wipes his eyes*)
> An angel passes through a house and leaves no imprint of his
> shadow on its wall. A man's life slowly changes and he does
> not understand the change. Things like this have happened
> before, and they can happen again. You understand, Jackson?
> You see what it is I'm saying?

JACKSON

You making a mole hill out of a mountain, sir. But I think I
follow you. You know what all this make me decide, pardner?

HARRY

What?

(JACKSON *picks up the umbrella, puts on the goatskin hat*)

JACKSON

I going back to the gift that's my God-given calling. I benignly
resign, you fire me. With inspiration. Caiso is my true work,
caiso is my true life.
 (*Sings*)
Well, a Limey name Trewe come to Tobago.
He was in show business but he had no show,
so in desperation he turn to me
and said: "Mr. Phillip" is the two o' we,
one classical actor and one Creole,
let we act together with we heart and soul.
It go be man to man, and we go do it fine,
and we go give it the title of pantomime.
La da dee da da da
dee da da da da da . . .
 (*He is singing as if in a spotlight. Music, audience applause.*
 HARRY *joins in*)
Wait! Wait! Hold it!
 (*Silence: walks over to* HARRY)
Starting from Friday, Robinson, we could talk 'bout a raise?

(Fadeout)